FAMILY GROW
ELECTIVES

Parenting Alone

Studies for Single Parents

Ramona Warren

David C. Cook Publishing Co., Elgin, Illinois—Weston, Ontario

Parenting Alone
© 1993 David C. Cook Publishing Co.

Scripture quotations, unless otherwise noted, are from the *Holy Bible, New International Version* (NIV). © 1973, 1978, 1984 by International Bible Society. Used by permission of Zondervan Publishing House.

Portions of this book and resources (1B, 2B, 2C, 3C, 4A-Part I, 4B, 5A, 5B, 6B, 7B, 7C, 8A, 9A, 10A, 10B, 11B, 11C, 12A, 12C, 13A, and 13D) are based on *Just Me and the Kids: A Course for Single Parents* by Patricia Brandt with Dave Jackson. © 1985 Patricia Brandt with Dave Jackson. Published by David C. Cook Publishing Co.

850 N. Grove Ave., Elgin, IL 60120-2892
Cable address: DCCOOK
Cover designer: Tom Schild
Cover illustrator: Pete Whyte
Illustrator: Julian Jackson
Desktop published by Dave and Neta Jackson
Printed in U.S.A.

ISBN: 0-7814-5064-1

Contents

Welcome to Family Growth Electives

Congratulations! The fact that you are using a study in the Family Growth Electives series says that you are concerned about today's families. You and your group of adults are about to begin an exciting adventure.

Each course in this series has been created with today's families in mind. Rather than taking a single topic and applying it to all adults, these Family Growth Electives treat each adult life stage separately. This means that people who are approaching or going through similar stages in life can get together to share and study their common needs from a biblical perspective.

The concept of family life stages comes from the work of Dr. Dennis B. Guernsey, associate professor of Marital and Family Therapy, Fuller Theological Seminary. Guernsey says that the family has critical tasks to accomplish at each stage in order to nurture healthy Christians.

Many adults in churches today have not come from strong Christian roots. Others may have attended church as children, drifted away during their adolescent or young adult years, and are now back in church in an effort to get help with the everyday problems of family life.

Some adults do not have the benefits of living near their extended family. The church can meet the needs of such people by becoming their "family." It can also help strengthen families by teaching them biblical principles and giving opportunities for applying those principles. That's exactly what you'll be doing as you lead your group in this Family Growth Electives study.

Terri Hibbard, Editor

Introduction

This course is for single parents—regardless of their children's ages. It deals with personal and family issues that single moms and dads face each day. Your group members will learn biblical principles they can apply to their particular family circumstances.

Parenting is one of the most difficult and rewarding challenges that adults face. Single parenting is an even greater challenge. In most cases, the custodial parent works full time and has total responsibility for the daily care of his or her children. This can be a lonely and scary reality.

This course will help single parents deal with loss and broken dreams, day-to-day aspects of raising children, and realistic expectations for the future. Your group members will learn many helpful tips about family life as they participate in the active learning in this course. You'll find activities for group members to do alone, in pairs, in small groups, and with the entire group together.

As the leader, you will find this course easy to prepare and use. Each forty-five- to sixty-minute session includes step-by-step instructions printed in regular type. Each session begins with "Getting Ready," listing everything you need to do before group time.

All content is Scripture based. At the beginning of each session plan you will find a list of the Scriptures to be covered. There are suggested time frames for each step of the lesson plan.

Things you might say aloud to your group are in **bold type**. Of course, it is always best to restate things in your own words. Suggested answers to questions are in parentheses.

Each of the thirteen sessions has reproducible resource sheets. In most cases you will use these as handouts for group members. It would also work to turn some resources into overhead transparencies, if you'd like.

Children are gifts from God. By using this Family Growth Elective, you will help your group members strengthen their family even though they are *Parenting Alone.*

Who Are We?

1

Session Aim:
To help single parents identify
and dispel negative labels
they give themselves and feel
others give them.

Single parents have left behind the once expected norm of one husband, one wife, and the children of this one and only marriage. These men and women are single for a variety of reasons which can be grouped into two categories—by choice or through circumstances beyond their control.

We all know single parents. They are in our community, our church, our neighborhood, and our family. In a day-care class of twenty preschool children, it is not unusual for one-half to three-quarters of the parents to be parenting alone. We work with these single parents, go to church with them, visit with them, and sometimes wonder how they manage. It isn't easy being single and a parent. Besides all the practical things they face each day, single moms and dads also feel their single status has automatically labeled them with a number of labels that are less than attractive.

This first session will help your group members identify and deal with any negative stereotypes they face. This material will help single parents begin to know themselves as complete and unique individuals who are able to meet needs and goals set by themselves and not others. It will also encourage them to gain God's perspective.

Single moms and dads often feel that their single status automatically tags them with less than attractive labels.

Getting Ready

Scriptures:

Proverbs 23:7; Philippians 4:8, 9; Isaiah 41:13; Galatians 6:2; Psalm 68:19; James 1:9, 17; Ephesians 6:9, 10; 4:2; Psalm 139:14.

1. Prepare enough copies of "Course Overview" (RS-1A—fill in dates before reproducing), "Single Stories" (RS-1B), and "Sticky Situation Studies" (RS-1C).
2. Provide work areas with collage-making supplies—large sheets of white paper or poster board, marking pens, and masking tape. Cut Bible verses from old curriculum materials, devotional books, calendars, or verse-a-day cards.
3. Have ready a simple drawing to introduce you and your family to the group. It will be an example of what the parents will do during the session. See Step 1 for directions.
4. Consult with your pastor and others to create a poster titled, "Resources for Families." List names and addresses of qualified counselors, other helping agencies, and inexpensive, fun activities for families.
5. Optional: small prize for the parent with the most family pictures.
6. For all sessions have available a chalkboard and chalk or newsprint and marking pens; extra Bibles and pens/pencils.

❶ Getting to Know You

Objective:

To help group members get acquainted with you and the other single parents in the group (10 minutes).

Welcome parents and ask them to search their purses or wallets to see how many pictures of their family members they have with them. At this point, don't get involved in introductions of the children. There will be time for that later. You may want to award a small prize—package of gum, coupon for film developing at a local store, etc.—to the person with the most family pictures!

Introduce yourself by showing the drawing you've prepared of your family. Divide the group into teams of two or three and move to the prearranged work areas around the room. Encourage them to gather with people they know least.

Write the following questions on the board or newsprint or on 3" x 5" index cards (one for each group).

1. What is the makeup of your household? Who lives with you?
2. What life experience brings the most joy to your task of parenting?
3. What family experience or situation is most challenging for you?

Help your group members identify and deal with any negative stereotypes they face.

Give each group a large sheet of newsprint or poster board, and have each person in the group work on a section of the paper. Each parent should answer the questions with simple drawings or phrases which represent his or her household. Each parent should put his or her family name in large letters by the appropriate illustration. Ask each one to choose a Bible verse for his or her family and write the reference in the same section.

Encourage the participants to consult with their team members for ideas to represent their families. This will help them to get better acquainted.

As the parents work, circulate around the room, talking with and encouraging them. Use this opportunity to begin getting better acquainted with each parent, family situation, and perhaps some of the special concerns.

Keep within the time limit for this activity, which may mean concluding the exercise even if some parents are not completely finished with their illustration.

With the whole group back together, have each small group hold up and explain their sheet. As this is being done, summarize some of the variations, qualities, and issues which appear in the illustrations. Encourage everyone to take a closer look at all the drawings after the session.

NOTE: Keep these sheets for reference in creating the group notebook "Parenting Joys and Struggles" for the next sessions.

❷ Looking Ahead

Objective:
To provide an overview of the course and a list of helpful resources for single parents (5 minutes).

Hand out copies of "Course Overview" (RS-1A). Briefly preview the course, noting the dates for the subsequent sessions. Ask which topics sound the most helpful to the parents. Keep this in mind as you plan future sessions.

Draw attention to the poster "Resources for Families" and encourage parents to contact and use the resources listed on it. Some may be aware of other resources not listed—encourage them to add this information to the poster. Ask participants to bring a Bible, notebook, pen or pencil, and the resource sheets from previous sessions to each session. Allow a minute for questions, then move on to the next activity.

Unfortunately, the Norman Rockwell picture of the traditional American family is increasingly rare.

❸ Removing the Labels

Objective:
To help participants identify and discard the negative stereotypes which are often associated with single parents (10-15 minutes).

What are some of the ways that single-parent households are produced? List each response on the board or newsprint. If any of the following are not mentioned, add them to the list:

- divorce
- marital separation
- illness or death
- prolonged business away from home
- adoption by singles
- choosing to raise a child born outside of a marriage relationship
- abandonment

Households headed by single parents are becoming more common. Based on the total number of children in the United States, just about one in eight (11.2 percent) lived in single parent homes in 1970; twenty years later the figure stood at more than one in five (20.2 percent) and was rising.[1] Thinking in terms of the total number of U. S. households, 9 percent are headed by single parents—7 million by a woman and 1.6 million by a man—according to Census Bureau figures for 1990. There are 3,200,000 children living with grandparents![2]
Unfortunately, the Norman Rockwell picture of the traditional American family is increasingly rare. We need to deal with the realities of our lives. One of these realities is the labels commonly associated with single parents. We do not have to look far to realize that many of these stereotypes are negative.
Ask three volunteers to each read one story from "Single Stories" (RS-1B).

What are some other labels or stereotypes that are associated with single parents? Add any of the following not already listed:

- shattered
- angry, depressed
- looking for a partner
- hard to get along with
- needy
- incompetent
- inadequate
- starved for romance
- poor or impoverished
- having trouble with children
- incomplete

L abels—both negative and positive—often shape our feelings about ourselves and, ultimately, our behavior.

Ask the group members to silently review the labels, identifying any with which they may be dealing. After a minute or two, take down the newsprint listing and crumple it or erase the board.

Let's remove all these labels and look to the Scriptures for a healthy way to deal with them.

❹ We Are What We Think

Objective:
To help parents replace negative labels with the truth of God's word
(10-15 minutes).

It is important to realize that labels—both negative and positive—often shape our feelings about ourselves and, ultimately, our behavior.

Ask someone to read Proverbs 23:7a aloud from the King James Version. ("For as he thinketh in his heart, so is he.")

Keeping the concept of labels in mind, how would you rephrase this verse? ("As one labels oneself, that is what one becomes.")

There are many negative labels floating around about how bad it is to raise children in a single-parent family. Magazine articles, news programs, and television shows all seem to suggest that single parenting is most likely to result in troubled kids.

We can't easily help what society tells us, but the real damage occurs when we internalize those messages and tell them to ourselves. This mindset leaves something essential out—the power of God at work in the family.

Our efforts must be to direct our thoughts in more positive, biblical directions.

Ask group members to find and read Philippians 4:8 to themselves. Tell them to reflect in three minutes of silent prayer on how the verse speaks to them personally—perhaps with a specific instance in mind. Then have them turn to one or two people next to them and tell what they thought about during the time of reflection.

Bring the group back together.

To focus our thoughts on God's Word, to dwell or to meditate on His truth, is also to pray. But keep in mind that Paul continues in verse 9 and expands upon his advice.

Ask someone to read Philippians 4:9. **What is Paul saying**

W hat is true in a given situation depends on two things—the actual reality and what God thinks of the situation.

here? (He tells the Philippians to begin doing the things that he has taught them. If they do, God's peace will be with them.)

Does this principle—obedience brings God's peace—apply to us too? (Yes!)

Paul wrote that we are to let our minds dwell on the things that are right and true. What is true in a given situation depends on two things—the actual reality and what God thinks of it.

First, let's practice identifying truth in terms of actual facts about a given situation. Pretend that you are the single parent in this situation: Your daughter Jessica can't find her shoes as the school bus approaches, and your car won't start, making you late to work for the third time this week. Last night there was last-minute homework as the clock crept toward 11 P.M., and today's potentially clean clothing remains piled by the washer. The child-support check is late when the grocery money is already stretched, and the lost shoes were never found, making it necessary to buy new ones.

Name any positives you notice. (You have a job, you have a car, there are still enough clean clothes to get by, lost shoes give an opportunity to teach responsibility.)

Identify one of the minuses and give a possible solution. (Lost shoes—take off shoes by the door when you come in; dirty laundry—start laundry before doing anything else; last-minute homework—check homework following dinner; car problem—find someone at church who works on cars; short on grocery money—let the family help you think of ways to have one or two low-cost meals.)

Dwelling on positive, effective responses to family issues may be an important key to overcoming the negative labels which can loom over us when times are tough. It might even be effective to actually imagine yourself handling those sticky situations of single parenthood with an exciting self-confidence. One single parent has the words, "We will make it through these tough times" printed on a note on the bulletin board in the kitchen where everyone in the family can read it. It's another way of saying, "This, too, shall pass." These thoughts coupled with God's promise of help give confidence.

welling on positive, effective responses to family issues may be an important key to overcoming the negative labels.

❺ Seeing with Eyes of Faith

Objective:
Help parents identify and claim some truths in God's Word that they can apply to current real-life situations (10-15 minutes).

Ask someone to read Isaiah 41:13 aloud. **What is the promise in this verse?** (God is with us and will help us.)

Hand out copies of "Sticky Situation Studies" (RS-1C) and have the parents get into groups of no more than five. If you have both men and women, assign Study 1 to the men and Study 2 to the women. Ask them to read and discuss the situation and Scriptures. Allow five to eight minutes for small group discovery.

Have volunteers report the findings of each small group.
Study 1:
(1. Pablo probably feels inadequate, helpless, alone, or discouraged.

2. Pablo could ask a female friend or youth leader from church to take his daughter shopping [Gal. 6:2]. He needs to remember that God is with him [Ps. 68:19]. He does not need to feel embarrassed [Jas. 1:9]. He does not have to give in to the temptation to be discouraged [Eph. 6:9, 10].)
Study 2:
(1. Andrea may feel embarrassed, humiliated, irritated at the person who suggested sending the food basket. She may feel inadequate.

2. She needs to be willing to let others help her so that they can function as God intends [Gal. 6:2]. She needs to recognize that she is not alone [Ps. 68:19]. She can receive the food as a gift from God [Jas. 1:17]. She can rely on God to keep her from being irritated [Eph. 6:9, 10]. She should be patient with those who are trying to help her [Eph. 4:2]. She has no need to be ashamed [Jas. 1:9].)

Ask parents to jot down in the space provided on the resource sheet one situation they are facing right now. Allow two or three minutes for parents to think of ways to replace wrong thinking with God's Word.

If time allows, have volunteers share their situations and have the group offer other verses they have found helpful.

Close the session by having the parents read aloud Psalm 139:14 as a prayer.

Notes:

1. Jerry Falwell, *The New American Family* (Ft. Worth, Tex.: Word, 1992), 7.

2. Christine Yount, "Meeting the Needs of Today's Families," *Children's Ministry Magazine*, November/December 1992, 6.

This Is My Life—Now

2

Session Aim:
To help the single parents learn self-acceptance and acceptance of life's present situation by rebuilding an adequate and positive self-identity.

Single parents are single—but not alone. This is frightening and challenging. First must come an acceptance of their situation and the responsibilities and priorities that are now in their lives. Along with this realization they can echo the Psalmist, "I love you, O Lord, my strength. The Lord is my rock, my fortress and my deliverer; my God is my rock, in whom I take refuge. He is my shield and the horn of my salvation, my stronghold. I call to the Lord, who is worthy of praise, and I am saved from my enemies. . . . In my distress I called to the Lord; I cried to my God for help. From his temple he heard my voice; my cry came before him, into his ears" (Ps. 18:1-3, 6).

Knowing Jesus as personal Savior is a single parent's greatest resource for improving his or her self-identity. The assurance of belonging to God—of being part of His family—helps remove the fear from scary circumstances and gives support during the challenging times.

Accepting and believing these truths is the first step singles must take toward accepting themselves and where they are right now.

K

Knowing Jesus as personal Savior is a single parent's greatest resource for improving his or her self-identity.

Getting Ready

Scriptures:
Philippians 4:8, 9; Psalm 139:1-6, 13-16, 23, 24.

1. A large newsprint pad, an easel to put it on, and colored markers to create a group notebook. Prepare this ahead of class with the title, "Parenting Joys and Struggles." Then list two or three *Joys of Parenting* (in one color) and two or three *Struggles of Parenting* (in a contrasting color). Use information from the introduction sheets parents made in the last session.
2. Enough copies of "Self-Portrait" (RS-2A), "The Identity-Building Cycle" (RS-2B), and "Me and My Self-Esteem" (RS-2C).
3. Business size envelopes.

❶ Parenting Joys and Struggles Notebook

Objective:
To allow group members to share and pray about their personal ups and downs as single parents
(10-15 minutes).

Welcome group members to the session and have them take turns telling their first names and something positive about themselves. Suggest they begin the sentence about themselves with words such as "I am (generous)"; "I can do (just about anything mechanical)"; "I know (how to roller blade)"; "I like (historical novels)"; etc. They can say whatever they want about themselves as long as it is positive. Begin by saying your name and something positive about yourself.

Introduce the group notebook of "Parenting Joys and Struggles" which you have prepared ahead of time. Explain that the notebook will be kept throughout the course in a location allowing for easy access by participants before and after the sessions. Encourage parents to add to it on a regular basis so that it will become a diary of group prayer and praise. Ask parents to list joys in one color (any bright color that is easy to read) and struggles in another color (dark blue or purple).

Invite parents to contribute some additional joys and struggles, particularly from the present week's experience. Take only a few minutes.

Ask someone to read the Scripture used in the last session—Philippians 4:8 ("Finally, brothers, whatever is true, whatever is noble, whatever is right, whatever is pure, whatever is lovely, whatever is admirable—if anything is excellent or praiseworthy—think about such things.") Pray together, encouraging several people to offer brief sentence prayers of praise to God for His faithfulness, even in times of difficulty.

*O*ne could even say that our self-identity is the combination of the labels we attach to ourselves."

❷ Here's Looking At Me!

Objective:
To help parents describe some components of their self-identity and learn ways that it can develop and change (10-20 minutes).

Distribute copies of "Self-Portrait" (RS-2A) and ask group members to look at Part I to help them see labels as a major source of self-identity.

According to authors Patricia Brandt and Dave Jackson, "Our self-identity is the picture we have of ourselves as we look at the many different facets of our lives. One could even say that our self-identity is the combination of the labels we attach to ourselves."[1]

What words would you use to describe yourself—to tell who you are?

Ask group members to work independently to add labels for themselves on their paper doll person. Point out that labels and identity categories are not always neatly packaged. Overlap and inconsistency are normal. Also note that some labels are more important than others. Make sure that the group knows to skip Part II for now.

Take three to five minutes and have parents turn to someone nearby and share their labels.

Read aloud this quote from Brandt and Jackson:

"Self-identity is formed early in life as we adopt what other people reflect to us about ourselves. Parents, family, teachers, the media, and other significant people in our life all have a part in shaping our identity. Even our life experiences and how we respond to them are a source of our identity. This is normal and natural. However, this is not the end of the identity story. We also shape our own identity through a process of risking and growing" (15).

Give participants a copy of "The Identity-Building Cycle" (RS-2B). Have them get into groups of two or three to read the steps and share examples.

After eight to ten minutes, bring the group together. **In this identity-building process new labels create new responses which in turn expand self-knowledge. And growth can continue. Let's see how God helps us lay the foundation for a new identity.**

*O*ur self-esteem is how much value we place on ourselves. It is the bottom line, the sum of the labels and how we feel about them."

❸ Put On the New Self

Objective:
To help single parents discover a scriptural base for a positive self-identity (10 minutes).

Ask three parents to read aloud the following three Scripture passages: Psalm 139:1-6, verses 13-16, and verses 23, 24. Have them look at Part II of "Self-Portrait" (RS-2A). Give each person an empty envelope.

Ask parents to think about the Bible passages they have just heard and write responses to the questions under "A Memo to Me." After about eight minutes ask parents to fold the sheet of paper and put it in the envelope. Use one of these two options:

1. Have each person put his or her name on the envelope, seal it, and give it to you. Assure the group that the envelopes will remain sealed until they are used again at a later time. (You may wish to leave the envelope open to add material from Step 4.)
2. Have group members address the envelope to themselves. You will mail it to them prior to Session 12.

❹ Enhancing Self-Esteem

Objective:
To help single parents identify ways of building a more positive self-esteem (10-15 minutes).

"If our self-identity is made up of the various labels we see for ourselves, then our self-esteem is how much value we place on ourselves. It is the bottom line, the sum of the labels and how we feel about them. Enhancing self-esteem is a process of changing self-labels. Three commitments are key to this change process" (Brandt and Jackson, 16).

Hand out copies of "Me and My Self-Esteem" (RS-2C). For additional variety and involvement, ask three members of the group to take turns reading the three "Keys to Change" in Part I.

They involve (1) recognizing that esteem building is a lifelong process, (2) being willing to risk new experiences, and (3) being willing to share ourselves, our feelings, our victories, and our defeats with at least one other person in a warm and affirming relationship of mutual support. Reinforce these concepts by asking parents to look at Part II. Have group members evaluate themselves on each method of building esteem, mark the scales at the appropriate places, and write a goal for growth in one or more areas.

Ask the group members to close in sentence prayers for the person to their right. Before praying, ask each person to repeat the positive thing he or she shared at the beginning of

Recognize that esteem-building is a lifelong process.

the session. Suggest that if someone does not prefer to pray aloud, he or she may pray silently and then say "Amen" aloud. Start the prayer time by thanking God for the person on your right and the positive thing he or she mentioned. Continue around the room until all have prayed.

Close the prayer session by praying for any requests that were recorded in the group notebook.

Notes:

1. Unless otherwise noted, materials by Patricia Brandt and Dave Jackson are quoted from *Just Me and the Kids* (Elgin, IL: David C. Cook Pub. Co.), 1985. All references in this text include the page number in that book. This quote is from page 15.

Healing Old Wounds

3

Session Aim:
To help single parents understand the stages of the healing process and to identify ways they personally can progress in their own healing.

Whether one is a single parent through death or divorce or through the experience of birth or adoption for a never-married parent, feelings of failure or rejection are common. These feelings are strong blows to the person's self-image. Betty N. Chase offers the following suggestions for developing a positive self-image:

1. Begin with a personal relationship with Jesus Christ.
2. Seek to grow as a Christian.
3. Renew your mind by reading Scripture every day.
4. Take action to change your life in accordance with instructions from God's Word every day.
5. Don't let guilty feelings defeat you. (Satan would like Christians to maintain an underlying feeling of guilt because it will rob them of joy and honesty as they relate to others.)
6. Be open and honest with yourself, others, and also with your Father as you talk to Him daily.
7. Develop several close or intimate friendships.
8. Analyze your negative tendencies (worry, judgmental attitudes, poorly expressed anger, etc.) and work towards eliminating them from your life-style by reading resources to help you.
9. Seek professional counseling with a competent Christian counselor if your self-image has been greatly damaged from childhood experiences.[1]

*I*t takes time to work through the blow to one's self-image that can come from the experience of becoming a single parent.

Getting Ready

Scriptures:
II Samuel 18:19-33; John 11:17-32; I Samuel 1:1-8; Job 42: 10-17; Psalms 16:1, 11; 94; 30; 118.

1. Group Notebook, "Parenting Joys and Struggles."
2. Sheets of paper—one for each person with the words, "Loss and Separation, Anger and Guilt" printed at the top.
3. Package of gum or other small prize for activity in Step 1.
4. Prepare enough copies of "What Happened?" (RS-3A), "Beth's Story" (RS-3B), and "Here I Am, Lord" (RS-3C).
5. Four different colors of chalk or marking pens.

❶ Negative to Positive

Objective:
To have single parents begin thinking about changing negative circumstances into positive growth (10 minutes).

Have the group notebook in an accessible place as parents enter, and encourage them to read it and make additions to it.

Give each person a copy of the paper with the words **"Loss and Separation, Anger and Guilt"** printed on the top or write the words on the board and provide paper and pencils. Ask each one to make as many POSITIVE words as possible out of the letters in the phrase. Tell parents that for each new word they may use each letter in the phrase only as many times as it appears in the phrase. For example, there are a total of three Ns, but only one D. Therefore any given word can include only one D, but up to three Ns.

Allow from two to five minutes. Some of the possible positive words include:

angel	Lord	sister
art	nap	sleep
aunt	nature	son
dine	orange	song
diner	pal	spare tire
dinner	parent	spire
gala	pear	spirit
great	rain	sponge
guest	rest	spring
lap	sail	tip
leap	sale	top
lilt	sing	

Select the winner by either of these options:

1. The person with the most *positive* words wins. Have this person read his or her list of words and offer your congratulations as you award the small prize.

2. Have each person read his or her list while all group members cross off any words they have in common with the reader. Continue this method until all lists have been read.

Losses like the breakup of a marriage, the loss of a spouse, and the loss of our identity as a married person require a grief process.

The person with the most *unique, positive* words is the winner.

Read the original negative words aloud again. **Before we look at the feelings involved in these negative words that we changed, let's pray together.**

Lead the group in prayer, thanking God for answers that have been recorded in the group notebook and praying about concerns that are listed.

❷ Loss and Healing Stages

Objective:
To help single parents understand the process of handling loss and the emotions which are a part of the healing process (20-25 minutes).

Authors Brandt and Jackson tell us, "When someone we dearly love dies, we expect to grieve. Some societies face the need for this more directly than others, and they have elaborate traditions for helping the bereaved person go through this process. Unfortunately, our western society tends to rush or ignore people's need for this process.

"Worse, we fail to realize that the same need for grieving accompanies other losses like the breakup of a marriage, the loss of a spouse and companion, and the loss of our identity as a married person. Even moving to a new neighborhood can trigger the same symptoms of a need to grieve that are evident when a loved one dies" (17, 18).

To discover these symptoms, let's look in on two single parents. As you hear each story, jot down the feelings or responses of the people involved.

Give two volunteers copies of "What Happened?" (RS-3A) to read aloud.

Ask participants to tell the feelings they have written down. As each emotion is named, list it on the board or sheet of newsprint, grouping the emotions into four numbered columns that will be labelled Denial, Anger, Depression, and Acceptance. DO NOT label the columns at this time. The list should include:

Denial	Anger	Depression	Acceptance
numbness	anger	waves of despair	forgiveness
bewilderment	hatred	no productivity	healing
disbelief	sense of betrayal	fear of future	
guilt		self-doubt	
		rejection	

Denial—for a time—is not all bad. It dilutes the full reality of a loss while we muster our emotional forces to cope.

As time allows, ask group members to describe their experience of loss through death, separation, or divorce and the impact it had on them. Add to the list any descriptions given in their stories that are not on the list. Point out the difference between grieving that has closure in the case of death of a spouse and ongoing grieving through separation or divorce.

These responses fall into four different categories. They are denial, anger/bargaining, depression, and acceptance. Much of our understanding about the stages of loss and grief come from secular research by Elisabeth Kübler-Ross. Several Christian books also deal with the grief process, including *Mourning into Dancing* **by Walter Wangerin, Jr.** (Zondervan) **and** *Choosing Joy* **by Tim Hansel** (David C. Cook Publishing Co.).

Before we decide where each response goes, let's take a closer look at each category.

Ask participants to form four groups. Hand out copies of "Beth's Story" (RS-3B). Assign one part of the story to each group. Ask them to read and identify which stage the person is in. Have them read the Scripture for each part and note parallels.

Call the group back together and ask them to report on their part of the story and the Scripture parallels. Add any other emotions to the list on the board.

II Samuel 18:19-33—(They both continued to exhibit hope in their circumstances—in a sense, denying the reality. Beth, and probably the children, too, knew their husband and father would not be coming back but did things to make it seem like he might; King David perhaps knew his son was dead but kept expressing the hope that the messengers were bringing him good news.)

John 11:17-32—(Beth and Martha were grieving and had begun questioning God. They both were angry at their circumstances.)

I Samuel 1:1-8—(They both experienced a long period of depression. Beth went to counseling for help; Hannah talked to God in the temple.)

Job 42:10-17—(They both found new lives and began to feel strong as a result of what they had been through. They came to the point of being able to forgive those who hurt them.)

Depression slows us down so that we can eventually let go of the pain of the loss without burying the memory.

Label the four columns of emotions as shown above. Go over the list of additional emotions, using four different colors of chalk or marking pens to circle each response according to the category into which it falls.

❸ Where Am I?

Objective:
To help the single parent identify his or her position in the loss and grief process and ways to progress toward emotional health (10-15 minutes).

Distribute copies of, "Here I Am, Lord" (RS-3C). Ask participants to circle the stage which best describes them at the present time, and have them identify and list their typical behaviors in that stage. Allow approximately five minutes for this process.

Some may be resistant to identifying their current stage and responses; others may simply not know. Don't pressure anyone to complete the exercise. Continue with the work sheet by reviewing the suggestions in the "Healing Helps" sections.

Underscore the idea that all stages are normal and natural, and, that sometimes you revert back to earlier stages for a time before progressing again. In fact, all stages are needed for true healing and for the release to take place. For example:

- **Denial is a protective device. It dilutes the full reality while we muster our emotional forces to cope with the loss.**
- **Anger/bargaining helps us to separate.**
- **Depression helps us to explore the full impact of the loss. It slows us down so that we can eventually let go of the pain of the loss without burying the memory and the influence of the lost relationship in our own lives and those of our children.**
- **Acceptance allows a special time when it is okay to explore new options without thinking that it is "high time that we settle down" again.**

Ask parents to look at each of the passages from Psalms and write a prayer in the area marked on the resource sheet using some of the thoughts the Psalmists used to express their feelings.

Acceptance allows a special time when it is okay to explore new options.

❹ Pair Prayer

Objective:
To help single parents affirm and support one another by listening and praying (5-10 minutes).

Have group members find a partner, and conclude the session with mutual sharing and prayer between these teams of two. If someone is without a partner, join this person to keep groups to only two.

Explain how this pair praying works: The first person prays for himself or herself. The second person listens. Then the second person prays for the first person and for himself or herself. Then the first person prays for the second person.

When it is time to dismiss, close your session with a prayer of thanks to God for His healing from past hurts.

Notes:

1. Betty N. Chase, *Discipline Them, Love Them* (Elgin, IL: David C. Cook Publishing Co., 1982), 34.

One Can Be A Lonely Number

4

Session Aim:
To help single parents make an honest assessment of their current level of independence and to accept responsibility to grow in competence.

Robert G. Barnes, Jr., in his book *Single Parenting*, likens the beginning of single parenting to wandering around in a wilderness—a wilderness of loneliness in terms of emotional climate and direction. His principles for walking out of the wilderness include:

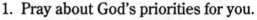

1. Pray about God's priorities for you.
2. Accept the responsibilities and priorities God has put before you.
3. Establish goals.
4. Commit yourself to these goals.
5. Knowing that God will help you to fulfill his priorities for your life, take the first step and keep walking.[1]

But possibly, before some of the single parents in your group are able to take the first step, they need to ask God to give them the *will* to walk out of the wilderness. The will to do is always a necessary part of the process. Sometimes we get so bogged down with the immediate, trying circumstances that we get used to them. It can become normal for us to live on the edge of crisis or from crisis to crisis.

With God, we can learn to put one foot in front of the other and day by day walk in His plan right out of the wilderness into what He has in mind for our lives.

With God, we can learn to put one foot in front of the other and day by day walk in His plan right out of the wilderness.

Getting Ready

Scriptures:
I Corinthians 10:13; Philippians 4:13; Ephesians 3:16; Colossians 1:11; Jude 24; Luke 18:27.

1. Group Notebook "Parenting Joys and Struggles."
2. Prepare enough copies of "This Is Reality" (RS-4A) and "First Steps Contract" (RS-4B).

❶ Accepting Reality

Objective:
To help single parents explore their feelings related to their independent status and role as head of household (10-15 minutes).

Be sure the "Parenting Joys and Struggles" group notebook is out so that parents may add to it as they come in.

Ask each parent to show something they have with them that indicates what they do as a single parent. As an example, suggest that a checkbook could represent being responsible for paying the bills.

Hand out copies of Part I of "This Is Reality" (RS-4A) for parents to fill in blanks and take notes as you continue. Read aloud the following material from Brandt and Jackson: (Words to fill-in are underlined.)

• **All of us from the time we were little children have been socialized to think of life—particularly family life— as something to be done in pairs. Thus, we feel a mixture of emotions when faced with the prospect of being a single parent/head of household.**

• **Our feelings range from bitterness and anger to fear and anxiety. For women especially, there is often a fear of success and competency. After all, isn't it risky to become too able to care for oneself? To be feminine is often thought of as needing to be cared for and protected. If these dependencies are gone, then what of the womanhood? If one does not need someone else, then maybe there won't be anyone else!**

• **Much the same is true for many men. The thought of making it alone is not pleasant, not normal, not desirable. And this is understandable. God did not intend family life to be handled by one parent alone. God said, "It is not good for man to be alone. I will make a helper suitable for him." And certainly the same is true for women, especially when their task is parenting.**

• **For those who have been married, the loss of husband or wife is not merely the loss of the companionship and support of a mate. It is a loss of a role or position—the position of wife or husband. As such, it is**

25

Even though single parenthood is not the ideal—not God's preference—it is the reality for many parents.

the loss of a major part of one's <u>self-identity</u> and often a source of one's <u>self-esteem</u>. Thus, the prospect of <u>building</u> a life alone and a family life as a single adult brings out all sorts of feelings.

• However, even though single parenthood is not the <u>ideal</u>, it is the <u>reality</u> for those of us in this group. And it is important to <u>embrace</u> it (21).

As Christians we can embrace this reality with the best possible help available. Let's take a look at where this help comes from.

❷ God Is Able

Objective:
To help the single parent discover biblical help in gaining competence (15-20 minutes).

Direct the group's attention to Part II of "This Is Reality" (RS-4A). Ask parents to circle the phrases with which they identify most. Have them list, in order of importance to them, the last three sentences of Thielicke's prayer.

Ask parents to get into groups of two or three according to how they ranked the items in the prayer. For example, those who ranked the first phrase as most important will form one group, those who ranked the second request as most important become another group, etc. Depending on the size of your group, you may have more than one group for each phrase. Give each subgroup one or more of the following verses: I Corinthians 10:13; Philippians 4:13; Ephesians 3:16; Colossians 1:11; Jude 24; Luke 18:27 to look up in their Bibles and paraphrase as they think of their situation as single parents. After a few minutes, have one person from each group read what he or she has written.

I Corinthians 10:13—(God is faithful to help us no matter what the temptation.)

Philippians 4:13—(God strengthens us for what we need to do.)

Ephesians 3:16—(God shares His power to strengthen us.)

Colossians 1:11—(God gives endurance and patience.)

Jude 24—(God can keep us from falling. He has joy in us.)

Luke 18:27—(Nothing is impossible with God.)

Ask parents to write on the back of the resource sheet the one assurance of God's help they have just heard that means the most to them.

Authors Brandt and Jackson encourage us with these words: "Perhaps God intends for you to more

God is faithful to help us no matter what our circumstances.

fully embrace the reality of your singleness and improve your competence—your abilities to do what needs to be done for yourself and your family" (21).

The fact that you are not part of a couple does not make you less competent or incompetent. Increasing your competency does not move you out of God's plan for you.

However, knowing that it is okay to increase competence and feeling secure enough about doing it may be two different things. Sometimes we need a plan to get us from where we are to where God wants us to be.

❸ Choosing a Plan

Objective:
To help single parents develop a personal plan for growth in competence (20-25 minutes).

Before the group members begin to work on their plans, read aloud the quote by Robert G. Barnes, Jr. from the introduction to this session.

Give out copies of "First Steps Contract" (RS-4B). In the same subgroups, have the parents work together on the first part of the sheet where they will identify areas in which they need growth.

Explain that the priorities they identify at the top of the page may or may not be areas needing growth. These areas are listed simply to keep them in mind as priorities. Without this clarification someone might be led to pursue a goal that interferes with a priority. For example, if a parent had a priority of putting an insecure child to bed each night because the child needed the personal attention, then it wouldn't be good to take an auto mechanics course which met three nights a week.

The remainder of the contract is self-explanatory, but encourage the parents to actually agree to be in contact with each other during the coming week.

Refer to the "Parenting Joys and Struggles" group notebook and mention the concerns and answers that have been added or review the concerns that still need prayer. If there are a number of concerns, give each group of two a concern to pray for as you close the session.

Notes:

1. Robert G. Barnes, Jr., *Single Parenting* (Wheaton, Ill.: Living Books, 1992), 47.

Helping Children Heal

5

Session Aim:
To equip parents so that they may help their children handle loss and grief in healthy ways.

A caregiver brought one of her four year olds into the day-care office because she thought he was running a fever. The thermometer showed 102.6°. As the caregiver began to call a parent, one of the directors asked, "When does his mother usually come to pick him up?"

The little boy responded matter-of-factly, "My mom died."

The director (besides feeling terrible about not remembering what had happened in this child's life) was surprised at how well he handled her question. It indicated to her that both family members and his caregiver in the school had helped him deal well with his loss.

The way children will react to a changed family structure will vary according to their ages and abilities to understand what is happening. It is important to help parents understand the different phases of loss their children may experience in order to help them. These guidelines will also help parents know what reactions are normal and best, as well as when it is necessary to get outside help.

Statistics tells us that children of divorced parents are more likely to have difficulty in school or in relationships when parents ignore their need for help in understanding what is happening to their family. But we must continue to remind single parents to remember that God is in charge and that they can depend on Him for direction.

The way children will react to a changed family structure will vary according to their ages and abilities to understand.

Getting Ready

Scriptures:
Psalms 9:9, 10; 27:1; 34:4; 46:1; 50:14, 15; 56:3, 4; 147:3; Matt. 5:4; 11:28; John 14:27; Romans 8:28; I Peter 5:7.

1. Group notebook "Parenting Joys and Struggles."
2. Enough copies of "Ways Kids Cope" (RS-5A), "Three Phases of Loss for Children" (RS-5B), "Lost and Found" (RS-5C), and "God's Promises for My Family" (RS-5D).
3. "Resources for Families" list which you prepared for Session 1.

❶ What's Happening to Us?

Objective:
To help single parents understand the process of loss for children (20-25 minutes).

Place the "Parenting Joys and Struggles" notebook near the door so that parents may easily add their prayer requests and answers.

Begin by having parents take turns telling something special their children have done for them—a gift they've made, something they've said or done that showed humor, caring, etc.

Share the following thoughts from authors Brandt and Jackson: **"Children are sensitive to our feelings and often respond by making, saying, or doing something that they hope will help us. Sometimes their responses are really requests to help them understand what's going on.**

"We can chart children's reactions to loss and separation from those they love more simply than for adults. For adults there are four or five distinct stages: denial, anger/bargaining, depression, and acceptance/rebuilding. For children the phases are usually: protest, anger, and hope."

Print these at the top of a chalk or marker board.

"This is where the simplicity ends. Undeveloped verbal skills of a child result in expressing experiences and emotions through their behavior. They act out their feelings—their emotional pain—in their day-to-day behavior" (23-24).

Ask parents to list what factors might affect a child's response to loss. Have someone write what is said on the board.

The list should include: parental response, age of child, availability of support systems, peer group, reaction of extended family, media, etc.

Point out that some responses may not surface for years.

"Children are sensitive to our feelings and often respond by making, saying, or doing something that they hope will help us."

As parents, we must carefully observe and interpret this behavior in order to understand how the child is coping with a separation or loss of a family member.

Hand out copies of "Ways Kids Cope" (RS-5A). Ask five volunteers to read the case studies aloud. After they are read, encourage parents to identify the behaviors which express different phases of loss. Record the group members' observations on the board under the three headings. Your chart should look something like this:

Child	Protest	Anger	Hope
Michael	Withdrawn during play Bedtime panic		
Jeff		Many accidents Frequent fights	
Tanya			Wants to face the loss Accepts the change
Mario	Covers ears Wants dad to return		
Samantha	Happy mom is gone Throws away mom's things	Plays role of mother	

When the observations have been recorded, distribute copies of "Three Phases of Loss for Children" (RS-5B), and ask three parents to each read aloud the explanation of one phase of the grief process for children.

Add any new reactions mentioned in the explanations to those already listed on the board. Take time to answer questions.

❷ Where Is Your Child?

Objective:
To help single parents identify how their own children cope with loss (5-10 minutes).

Distribute copies of "Lost and Found" (RS-5C) to each parent. If anyone has more than three children, give this person an extra copy of the handout. Ask parents to work on it alone, doing the portions relating to protest and anger.

Use this time to circulate around the room, assisting any parents who are having difficulty identifying specific behav-

Undeveloped verbal skills of a child result in expressing experiences and emotions through their behavior."

iors. Assure the parents that identifying the behavior is the important task. Assigning the behavior to a particular phase is secondary.

❸ Next Steps

Objective:
To provide single parents some suggestions of ways they can encourage the healing process within their families (10-15 minutes).

Ask parents to get into three teams based on where their oldest child is among the three stages of loss. Try to keep the teams limited to three or four people. If necessary, form more than one team for a particular phase.

Have parents brainstorm ways to help in each phase. After five to seven minutes reconvene the large group and have a recorder share insights. Affirm suggestions. If any of the following are not mentioned, add them to your list:

Protest:
* Maintain familiar routines without denying facts or emotions.
* Take time to talk of the loss with the children who are old enough to verbalize their feelings.
* Provide blankets, stuffed animals for cuddling; reinstate nighttime routines such as stories, rocking, night-lights, and quiet music appropriate to ages.
* Provide healthy snack foods and include more reassuring foods of younger days such as applesauce, mashed potatoes, etc., for poor appetites.
* Let children know when you need to be away from them, who will care for them while you are gone, and when you will return. Give older children a watch and expected time of return. Give younger children a key or other significant possession to care for while you are gone. This helps reassure your return. Always call children if you will be delayed.

Anger:
* When the child expresses his or her sadness and anger verbally or physically, take time to listen and take action as soon as it happens. The child needs priority attention.
* Use touching, holding, sitting close to reassure the child.
* Provide play experiences for rerunning the loss experience and releasing pent-up anger. Plenty of physical outlets with structure and redirection for aggressiveness deflect behavior from coming out in harmful ways.

• Make simple lists and reminders for the disorganized or hyperactive child. Use words for children who can read and pictures for younger children.

Hope:
• Be ready for when the child signals a willingness to say good-by.
• After the grieving, encourage new outlets and interests. Offer two or three choices of things the child would like, such as piano or swimming lessons or a new bike.
• Help the child keep old ties and memories, along with new relationships and experiences.
• Let children share in establishing new traditions.

One of the major concerns for all parents when their children are going through hard times is knowing whether or not their struggles are within the bounds of what is normal and manageable given the circumstances. They also need guidance on when the family needs professional help.

Refer parents to the bottom of RS-5C. Go over each point and invite discussion. Tell parents to use this material as guidelines for assessing their children's need for professional help in dealing with loss. Display the list of counseling resources that you shared in Session 1.

Encourage parents to complete the remainder of "Lost and Found" (RS-5C) at home by planning and attempting to carry out one helping strategy per child in the next week.

❹ The First Place To Look for Help

Objective:
To help single parents see Bible verses as a practical first step in finding help for the varied needs of their children (10-15 minutes).

Hand out copies of "God's Promises For My Family" (RS-5D) and assign one verse to each parent.

God's Word is filled with promises—promises from Him to you and your children. Each of these verses reminds us of one of His promises. Look up your verse and use it to write a prayer for your family.

After three to five minutes, have several volunteers read their verse and tell what meaning it has for them now. Affirm parents as they apply God's Word to their individual situations.

The general promise in each verse is listed below.

Psalm 9:9, 10—(God is our refuge and He doesn't forsake us.)
Psalm 27:1—(He is our light and stronghold.)

God's Word is filled with promises—promises from Him to you and your children.

Psalm 34:4—(He answers our prayers and delivers us from our fears.)

Psalm 46:1—(He is an ever-present help.)

Psalm 50:14, 15—(He delivers us when we call upon Him.)

Psalm 56:3, 4—(He is trustworthy.)

Psalm 147:3—(He heals the brokenhearted.)

Matthew 5:4—(He comforts those who mourn.)

Matthew 11:28—(He gives rest to those who are worn out.)

John 14:27—(He gives peace that lasts.)

Romans 8:28—(He works things together for good for those who love Him.)

I Peter 5:7—(He cares for me.)

Encourage parents to take the resource home, discuss with their children (if they are old enough) what each week's verse means, and write a prayer for their family. Suggest that parents put each week's verse and prayer on a 3" x 5" index card to display on a bulletin board or wall for family members to see during the week.

Close in prayer, remembering to mention answers to prayer and requests that are in the "Parenting Joys and Struggles" notebook.

Remaking Our World

6

Session Aim:
To help single parents learn ways to find and give affirmation.

Mel Krantzler, author and counselor, suggests that single parents give themselves positive messages, complimenting themselves for things they have done well, such as washing a floor. He also advises accepting compliments from others as "an honest expression of how at least one outsider views you."[1]

Other good words of advice include: Learn to treat yourself gently—your present feelings of abandonment, rejection, and failure will go away; keep away from people who like to lecture; think ahead about how to handle parties and holidays, and make other plans if necessary; do something physical such as walk or swim to alleviate stress, watch what you eat and drink; think about the different ways you can give yourself a treat such as time with friends, personal quiet time, shopping, or whatever.

Single parents need to feel good about themselves. It can make the difference between a happy person and one who is just existing—it affects all other areas of their lives. As one single parent said, "If I don't feel good about myself, no one else does either."

GRAND PRIZE WINNER
City Art Fair

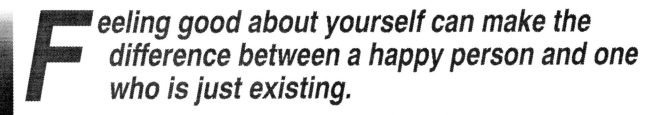

Feeling good about yourself can make the difference between a happy person and one who is just existing.

Getting Ready

Scriptures:
Psalms 37:3; 139:14; Jeremiah 31:3; John 3:16; Romans 5:8; Ephesians 2:4, 8, 10, 19; Colossians 1:10; II Thessalonians 2:17; Titus 2:14; 3:4,5; Hebrews 10:24; James 1:22-24.

1. Group notebook "Parenting Joys and Struggles."
2. Prepare enough copies of "A Slogan That Fits Me" (RS-6A) and "It's All in How You Say It!" (RS-6B).
3. Two 3" x 5" index cards with information from Step 2 written on them.
4. Optional: Newspapers and magazines.

❶ How One Feels Affirmed

Ojective:
To encourage single parents to remember recent experiences when they have felt affirmed (20 minutes).

Have the "Parenting Joys and Struggles" notebook ready to receive parents' entries. Open the session by giving parents the opportunity to pray together, thanking God for answers and asking help for concerns.

Hand out copies of "A Slogan That Fits Me" (RS-6A). Ask parents to choose one slogan that expresses how they feel on a good day. You might have some newspapers and magazines available for additional slogans. Be prepared to give one for yourself to start off.

Ask parents to think of something that happened recently that was positive and helped them to feel as good about themselves as the slogan they selected. Write the following questions on the chalk or marker board:

- **How, where, and why did the affirming experience take place?**
- **Specifically, how did it make you feel good?**
- **What was different about this experience that made it so good?**

Invite as many parents as time allows to respond to the first two questions by telling the experience that the slogan brought to mind. Ask the listeners to respond to the third question after each parent speaks.

If the group has little to tell about or if you have enough time, you might give the following examples of affirmation:

A single father found affirmation in church ministry. Through a gifts-testing seminar at his church, he was affirmed in his talent for building and doing repairs—which he also enjoys as a change from his weekday desk job. Ever since he let his interest and availability be known, he has had jobs lined up for repairs around the church facility and for other singles and older church members who think he's a "wonder" and "answer to prayer."

Holidays were difficult for a single mother in her thirties—especially the ones when her children spent time with their father. Those days were when she felt the biggest sense of failure that bordered on depression. Now she volunteers for local agencies that serve food to the homeless at Thanksgiving and Christmas. On other holidays she holds parties and picnics for other singles. She's met a lot of new people and feels good about the variety of ways she can help others. Her new friends appreciate being included in holiday plans too.

❷ I Hear You

Objective:
To help single parents understand and practice two elements in communicating affirmation (10-15 minutes).

As Brandt and Jackson remind us, **"Affirmation comes to us in many ways. Sometimes it is in the little things in our day-to-day experience, and sometimes it is the result of the larger sweeps in our life. . . . An affirming encounter may take place in a variety of settings and a number of ways. It can differ in its content in terms of words and ideas. However, it will usually contain two foundational elements"** (28).

Prior to group time, write the following two paragraphs on 3" x 5" index cards. Distribute them to two volunteers who will read them aloud.

FOCUSED ATTENTION begins and maintains affirming experiences. To focus attention, position your body to face the person. This tells the person that he or she is noticed and important because your attention is directed toward him or her. You can also focus attention with direct eye contact and touch.

FACILITATIVE MESSAGES contribute to affirmation. They encourage the communication process. The person receiving them feels he has been heard as the other person nods his head, restates feelings or issues in ways demonstrating understanding, or asks questions or requests further explanation rather than cutting off dialogue. Facilitative messages use words that affirm and encourage.

*W*e can give focused attention and facilitative messages without necessarily agreeing with all the other person has said."

According to Brandt and Jackson, "It is important to understand that we can give focused attention and facilitative messages without necessarily agreeing with all the other person has said. This is a time for communicating understanding, not debating differences" (28).

To reinforce these concepts, ask the parents to get into pairs. If someone is left out, you become that person's partner. Have one partner spend three to five minutes telling about an area of his or her life which currently lacks affirmation. Ask the other partner to practice focused attention and facilitative messages. Then have the teams exchange roles.

Ask the entire group: **How did you feel as you were sharing about your life? How did you feel as you listened and affirmed your partner?**

This may be a new experience for some of your group members. So don't be surprised if they feel a little awkward. Encourage them to use this technique with each other, their children, and friends.

❸ Strength Bombardment

Objective:
To help single parents discover a biblical model for affirmation (15-20 minutes).

The Lord affirms us continually in His Word. He affirms us both for who we are and for what we do.

Have parents stay in their groups of two and give each group two or three of the following Scripture passages to look up in their Bibles. It may be helpful to print the references on slips of paper to hand out.

Psalm 37:3—(doing)
Psalm 139:14—(being)
Jeremiah 31:3—(being)
John 3:16—(being/doing)
Romans 5:8—(being)
Ephesians 2:4—(being)
Ephesians 2:8, 19—(being)

Ephesians 2:10—(doing)
Colossians 1:10—(doing)
II Thessalonians 2:17—(doing)
Titus 2:14—(being/doing)
Titus 3:4, 5—(being)
Hebrews 10:24—(doing)
James 1:22-24—(doing)

Print the words "BEING" and " DOING" on the board. Ask parents to decide whether their passages affirm who they are—their being, what they do—their doing, or both. Have parents restate the passage in their own words to share with the whole group.

Just as God affirms us for being and doing, we need to learn to affirm others and ourselves in these two areas.

J ust as God affirms us for being and doing, we need to learn to affirm others and ourselves in these two areas.

In her book *Self-Esteem: A Family Affair*, Jeanne Clarke explains that affirmation skills can include rewards for simply being. We tell people they are lovable just the way they are. These messages are basic to the emotional nourishment process for us and our children.

Another kind of affirmation rewards what we accomplish. These are affirmations for doing. These rewards are needed to encourage and enhance self-esteem.

There is scriptural base for both types of affirmation, as shown in the passages we just reviewed.

Single parents may have a lack of affirmation in their homes. Even though children may appreciate what their mother or father does, they are neither observant nor mature enough to express it.

Where does the single parent receive the deserved affirmations for "doing"? (Friends such as those in this group, parents, co-workers, children.)

If it is not mentioned, point out that we can legitimately reward ourselves with small accomplishment promises: "When the kitchen is cleaned, I am going to sit down for ten minutes and read my book," or, "As soon as I meet my goal, I'm going to have an evening out to celebrate." Caution parents that the reward should be constructive and helpful. For instance, if they have trouble handling money, they'd better not treat themselves with an afternoon of shopping!

❹ Taking It Home

Objective:
To help the group members design a plan for building affirmation for themselves and their families (5-10 minutes).

Hand out copies of "It's All in How You Say It!" (RS-6B). As a group, go over the material.

Point out the three components on the resource sheet:

1. Messages which expand rather than constrict or cut off dialogue.
2. Messages which restate feelings and issues to reassure the other person that you are understanding.
3. Messages which affirm both being and doing.

Have the partners work together to write down and discuss their family members and the areas needing affirmation in their lives. Have each pair brainstorm and make note of any unique ways facilitative messages could be communicated.

As a goal, partners might also think of and write down

Affirmation skills can include rewards for simply being. We tell people they are lovable just the way they are.

times when they can affirm family members during the coming week. As time permits, ask volunteers to share their insights with the entire group.

What are some ways in which you might help your children learn to affirm you and each other? (Being an example is a good place to start; play games such as Life Stories [Standard Publishing Company] in which each person is affirmed when they reach the finish line. Practice focusing on the positive and catching your children being good.)

Close in prayer asking God to help parents receive the affirmation they need and give the affirmation their children need as they continue remaking their world.

Notes:

1. Quoted by Carol Vejvoda Murdock, *Single Parents Are People, Too!* (New York: Butterick Publishing, 1980), 21.

What Is the Family's Function?

7

Session Aim:
To help single parents understand the family as a social and emotional unit having important biblical functions.

James Dobson and Gary Bauer define the traditional family as "a group of individuals who are related to one another by marriage, birth, or adoption—nothing more, nothing less."[1] This simple definition is broad enough to include two-parent, single parent, adoptive, and blended families.

Dobson and Bauer further explain that traditionalists believe in: (1) lifelong marriage; (2) the value of bearing and raising children; (3) the traditional family that consists of individuals related by marriage, birth, or adoption; (4) the universal worth of each individual in the family, regardless of his or her productivity or other contributions; and (5) basic values, such as the importance of commitment to premarital chastity, self-discipline, hard work, fidelity, and loyalty between spouses.[2]

**A** family is *"a group of individuals who are related to one another by marriage, birth, or adoption—nothing more, nothing less."*

Getting Ready

Scriptures:
Ephesians 4:16; Colossians 3:12-14; I Peter 3:8, 9; Deuteronomy 11:18-21.

1. Group notebook "Parenting Joys and Struggles."
2. Prepare enough copies of "Family Portrait" (RS-7A), "What Is the Function?" (RS-7B), and "Building Blocks" (RS-7C).

❶ The Name Game

Objective:
To have group members reflect on the unique contribution each family member makes to their family (10 minutes).

As parents arrive, ask them to make any entries they would like in the group's "Parenting Joys and Struggles" notebook.

Give each person a sheet of paper and ask them to give a descriptive name to each person in the family (including themselves) using the first initial of first and last names. The name should indicate what the person contributes to the family. George Fox could be "generous friend" or "great fun lover." Come up with one for yourself as an example.

Ask the group members to share the names with the whole group.

We've begun thinking about what a family is by describing family members. Let's look at what the Bible says about the family.

❷ Family Functions

Objective:
To help single parents discover a biblical, functional approach to the family (15-20 minutes).

In her book, *What Is a Family,* **Edith Schaeffer builds a model of the family out of the simple concept of a mobile. Each person has a part to play, and yet each part is separate. There is relatedness and nurture, support and love, as the family acts and reacts together as a system. Yet there is also flexibility, independence, and a sense of separateness for each member. This would be a structural model of the family.**

Can you think of a structural model in the Bible? (The Body of Christ. If no one responds, ask someone to read Ephesians 4:16 where we are reminded that the whole body is "joined and held together by every supporting ligament, [and] grows and builds itself up in love, as each part does its work.")

We might even think of the family as a mini-church.

A structural approach is one way to look at a family. In this approach, each parent makes specific contributions based on roles of husband and wife. This approach presents problems for a single-parent family, because there aren't two parents to assign to different roles. An alternative way to look at the family is a func-

tional approach. The functional approach asks what functions or tasks the family should accomplish with all of its members.

Ask parents to get into three groups by counting off by threes. To Group One, assign Colossians 3:12-14; to Group Two, assign I Peter 3:8, 9; and to Group Three, assign Deuteronomy 11:18-21. Give each person a copy of "Family Portrait" (RS-7A). Have each group read the assigned passage that describes one of the three broad categories shown in the picture frames on the resource sheet. Ask the groups to brainstorm the specific ways families fulfill the function from their passage. After several minutes call the whole group together and follow up with these additional questions and comments:

Based on Colossians 3:12-14, what is the first function of the family? (To provide an atmosphere of <u>love and nurture</u>.) This is a safe place away from the tension and stress of the outside world. God intends the family to provide a sense of relatedness and care between each family member. Love, then, is the bond and mark of the Christian family.

It is out of this sense of relatedness that family members learn to handle relationships.

What things related to love and nurture do we learn in the family? (To care for children [new members], support one another, listen to one another, care for in sickness and difficulty, give and receive love, communicate needs, handle emotions, grapple with the urge for power and position, how to lead and follow. It is in the family that we begin to learn about servanthood.)

According to I Peter 3:8, 9, what is the second function of the family? (To provide <u>order and organization</u>, which give a sense of rootedness, place, and purpose.)

To establish order and organization, what does the Christian family need to do? (Provide discipline; encourage responsibility, appropriate roles, and biblical values; and teach how to pray, give, and worship.)

According to Brandt and Jackson, "The Christian family is to order its space, time, and energy as a model of excellence such that God will be glorified. In doing this the Christian family will also create a secure and predictable environment with which individual family members can identify, thereby enhancing the potential for their growth and development.

The Christian family is to order its space, time, and energy as a model of excellence such that God will be glorified."

"This sense of order and organization allows the family to socialize its members into specific life-style patterns—it reinforces family values. The final product is an independent, self-disciplined adult living out his or her values with freedom and conviction" (31).

According to Deuteronomy 11:18-21, what is the third function of the family? (To teach God's vision in a daily way.)

How does this function relate to teaching God's <u>vision for family</u> to our children? (This is one of the more challenging tasks for the single parent. Patiently take the time to discuss this task after the following introduction.)

God's ideal for the design of the family is to give every child a home with two parents, loving each other and loving the children. Unfortunately, as we all know, that ideal isn't always achievable. Being competent and trusting God to meet our needs is our primary task as single parents, and many times that requires affirming our family situation as okay.

However, in saying and believing that our family is "okay" and competent—with God's help—do we sometimes inadvertently pass on the message to our children that the single parent model is an option for them?

Even if we don't intend to give that message, society does it for us. In the media, the traditional two-parent family is portrayed at best as only one option among many and at worst as an out-of-date fantasy. Where two-parent families are noted at all, the Simpsons are "realistic," while the Cleavers are now called fakes. Educators and other child care workers avoid making our children feel bad by presuming that they have a mother and father at home. On one hand, that's considerate, but on the other hand, all this input can create a new "ideal" for the family.

In wrestling with this trend, African-American columnist William Raspberry notes that the most extensive research clearly shows "children of two-parent homes tend to be better off on almost every count: less likely to be poor or economically insecure, more likely to do well in school, less likely to become dependent adults, more likely to go to college, less likely to be involved in crime.

O

rder and organization allows the family to socialize its members into specific life-style patterns—it reinforces family values."

"We know all these things but hesitate to say them lest we appear to 'look down upon single parents as if it's some type of disease.' . . .

"The point is not that there's anything wrong with particular single mothers, or that they owe it to society to grab and marry the first available man. The point is to help the young not-yet parents understand what we know very well: that their children will be better off if mom and dad are both there, committed, full time. And we need to remind ourselves that the increase in the proportion of single-parent households is already changing our society in disturbing ways, with the clear prospect of worse to come. We know these things, and we need to find the courage to say them."[3]

So, how do we pass on the vision of the two-parent family when our own home does not model that ideal and when we sometimes struggle to prove to ourselves and our kids that we are "okay"? (We can deliberately teach the Bible's ideal for family. We can be sure our children spend time with relatives and friends [particularly in the church] where there is a father and mother in the home. We can be honest about the challenge and loneliness of being a single parent. We can be frank about the facts concerning advantages for children from two-parent homes. [One secular source is "Dan Quayle Was Right" by Barbara Dafoe Whitehead, *The Atlantic* magazine, April 1993.])

❸ Flexible or Fixed?

Objective:
To help single parents identify tasks the family is to accomplish through and for its members (10-15 minutes).

Distribute copies of "What Is the Function?" (RS-7B). Ask the group to divide into pairs. Assign various teams different passages from the resource sheet to look up. If each team has only three or four passages to find, there will be time to cover all the verses.

Tell the parents to also keep "Family Portrait" (RS-7A) nearby. It will help them identify the tasks and functions that they are looking for.

Have each team fill in the Key/Summary Word identifying the task described in the passage. Then have them check whether it is a Love-and-Nurture function, an Order-and-Organization function, or a Vision-for-Family function. The sample below suggests what the findings might be:

In proclaiming that our family is "okay," do we inadvertently pass on the message that the single parent model is a good option?

	Key/Summary Word	Love and Nurture	Order and Organization	Vision for Family
Gen. 2:24	Marriage			X
Exod. 20:12	Honor		X	
Deut. 6:1-7	Values		X	X
Deut. 24:5	Happiness	X		X
Psa. 68:3-6	Caring	X		X
Psa. 103:13	Compassion	X		X
Prov. 1:8, 9	Instruction		X	X
Prov. 4:1-4	Instruction		X	X
Matt. 19:4-9	Divorce			X
Col. 3:18-21	Order		X	X
Eph. 6:1-4	Consideration	X		X
I Pet. 3:1-8	Submission		X	X
I John 4:11, 12	Love	X		

Allow about five to seven minutes before asking the teams to share their findings with the whole group. Have group members fill in the findings of the other teams.

❹ Family Building Blocks

Objective:
To help single parents plan ways of building a sense of family for themselves and their children (10-15 minutes).

Ask parents to work in the same pairs as for the previous activity. Hand out copies of "Building Blocks" (RS-7C). Assign one or two topics with related questions to each group. Give the pairs five minutes to brainstorm answers. Reconvene the whole group and ask each pair to lead a short discussion on their topic and questions.

Following the discussion ask parents to refer to their creative family names from the opening activity and silently pray for each family member. Close this quiet time with prayer that mentions the concerns and praises in the group notebook.

NOTE: Have group members bring "Family Portrait" (RS-7A) to the next session.

Notes:

1. James Dobson and Gary Bauer, *Children at Risk* (Dallas, Tex.: Word Publishing, 1990), 57-58.
2. Ibid, 20.
3. William Raspberry, "The Conundrum of Single Parenthood," *Chicago Tribune*, April 12, 1993, Sec. 1, 15.

Great (but Realistic) Expectations

8

Session Aim:
To help single moms and dads set realistic parenting goals.

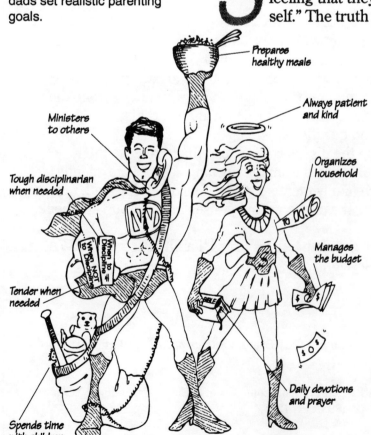

Prepares healthy meals

Always patient and kind

Ministers to others

Organizes household

Tough disciplinarian when needed

Manages the budget

Tender when needed

Spends time with children

Daily devotions and prayer

ingle parents need to accept that they are not Wonder Moms or Super Dads. They need to avoid the trap of feeling that they must and can "do it all—all by myself." The truth is—they can't. And if they try to do too much and set unrealistic goals they can become paralyzed or burn out. Single parents need to free themselves from the notion that they must be all things to their children, compensating for the lack of two parents in the household by being the perfect single parent.

Noted psychologist L.W. Osher offers this good advice, "We had to do fewer things or do some less well."[1]

Single parents need to keep these three things in mind: the actual reality; their most important priorities; their level of energy and stress.

*M*ost parents can describe the perfect parent, but none have ever met this person!

Getting Ready

Scriptures:
Ephesians 4:2; Psalm 27:1-3; Psalm 46:1-11; Isaiah 40:28-31; II Corinthians 12:9, 10.

1. Group notebook "Parenting Joys and Struggles."
2. Prepare copies of "Your Energy Bank" (RS-8A) and "Tough or Tender" (RS-8B).
3. Extra copies of "Family Portrait" (RS-7A) for those who do not have their copy with them.
4. A 3" x 5" index card for each parent.

❶ Parent Talk

Objective:
To have parents reflect on some of the positives of single parenting (5-10 minutes).

Make sure that parents know where the "Parenting Joys and Struggles" notebook is for any entries they would like to make. Before the session begins, pray together about the things listed in the book and thank God for answers to any requests that have been given. Make sure to record answers in the book.

What one thing do you do with your children that you enjoy most? Have all volunteers share, and affirm each contribution.

We've told the things that we like to do with our children. The problem usually is finding time to do them—so we can be the kind of parents we want to be.

❷ Perfect-Parent Message

Objective:
To help single parents identify "perfect parent" expectations that exist in their parenting goals (20-25 minutes).

Almost every parent desires the best for his or her child and wants to be as good a parent as possible. All of us have an image of what a good mother or father is supposed to be like. Dennis and Barbara Rainey call this our "phantom." They use the term "phantom" because most parents can describe the perfect parent, but none have ever met this person! Single parents may be even more prone to have "phantoms" than married moms and dads. We can overload ourselves very easily if we are not careful.

Authors Brandt and Jackson tell us that "we all have only so much energy. It is like a bank account. Energy must be invested and saved before it can be withdrawn and spent. If we overdraw our resources, we will often run into trouble—too often that trouble will be in the form of delivering a bill of blame and frustration to our children" (33-34).

Hand out copies of "Your Energy Bank" (RS-8A). Ask parents to fill out the sheet by identifying how much energy

> # **W**e all have only so much energy. Energy is like a bank account. It must be invested . . . before it can be withdrawn and spent."

each activity deposits in their "energy bank" and how much it takes out. They will find that some activities are almost entirely a drain—maybe that is true of enforcing rules—whereas other activities such as having daily prayer may take a little investment to schedule and accomplish but yield high returns in energy. For each activity, parents should indicate the energy drain or debit on a scale of "0" for no energy to "–3" for maximum debit and the energy return or credit on a scale "0" for no return to "+3" for maximum credit.

An example would be as follows: Under "earning a living" a parent may indicate that it takes the maximum energy debit of "–3." But there may be some important credits from the job because of the sense of affirmation for doing a job well. So one might score the credit column as "+1."

If a parent does not do certain things, like home maintenance, he or she might indicate the cost of getting someone else to do the job. If the task is outside their realm of experience, parents can rate it as two zeros.

Encourage parents to work through the paper rather quickly without reflecting long on any activity. First responses will probably be the most telling. Allow about five minutes to mark the Debit and Credit columns.

Have the parents determine the Net Result for each activity by adding the two columns together and recording the answer in the far right hand column. In the example above, the Net Result is –2.

After the Net Result is determined for each item, have parents add this final column. This will result in the final balance for each parent's energy bank. Having calculators available will speed this process! Emphasize that this is not a precise tool for telling parents that they are overextended or have extra energy, but it will help them to think about their balance.

Some parents will find themselves in the black, others will find themselves in the red—spending more energy than they receive. The goal is to break even, at least, or achieve a positive balance, at best. Encourage those with an energy debit to review their lists and plan ways of increasing activities that show a positive Net Result. Take time for group discussion and suggestions to encourage one another in ways to change the balance to a positive figure. Remind your group that some things that are essential may always take more than they give back. The trick is to offset these activities with others that restore energy.

❸ Perfect-Parent Patterns

Objective:
To help single parents identify patterns of compensation in which they attempt to make up for the missing parent (10-15 minutes).

There is often a compensation process that single parents participate in as they try to make up for the lack of two parents or the influence of the absent parent. This may or may not be a conscious effort.

Ask parents to brainstorm ways they may overcompensate and write them on the board. The list should include: toys, clothing, special excursions, extravagant gifts, time, balancing over/under indulgences of the other parent, overemphasizing limits.

Single parents often feel that their own needs must remain secondary to those of the children. But overindulgence in either the area of time or material things gives the child a false picture of life and will take its toll on the parent.

Maybe the other parent is an absentee parent who does not provide for the child's basic support but gives the child extravagant gifts that the custodial parent can't afford. The damage is in terms of the image of the custodial parent. The child may think that the absentee parent cares more than the custodial parent who is actually providing the primary support for the child.

The noncustodial parent may not provide the child with appropriate limits and discipline. This gives the child mixed messages and eventually leads to discipline problems that both parents must handle.

Hand out copies of "Tough or Tender" (RS-8B). Encourage the parents to use the sheet to list their children's names and identify ways in which they are "too tough" or "too tender" in their effort to compensate for the other parent.

Invite volunteers to share their insights with the group as they work through the resource sheet. Sharing as they go may help some parents think of areas they would have otherwise missed. Ask parents to use this sheet as a prayer guide during the week as they seek the Lord's help in this area of single parenting. Let them know that they will be taking a closer look at this area of single parenting in the next session.

*I*f the noncustodial parent does not provide appropriate limits and discipline, the child is likely to develop discipline problems.

❹ Super Help for Not-So-Super Parents

Objective:
To help parents who are feeling driven to fulfill unrealistic expectations by directing them to the Lord as their source of help (10 minutes).

Building a new identity as a single parent is certainly not an easy task. It is often made more difficult in Christian settings because of the subtle implication that a single parent family cannot successfully nurture and guide its children. Yet, while there are difficulties, single parents can competently provide a warm Christian environment in which children can mature (35).

On the chalkboard or newsprint list the following Bible references:

> Psalm 27:1-3
> Psalm 46:1-11
> Isaiah 40:28-31
> II Corinthians 12:9, 10

Ask volunteers to read the passages. As a group discuss how having the perspective of the Lord as our Helper can minimize or eliminate the compulsion to be a superparent. You might ask parents to choose the passage that most speaks to them and to read it each day for a week as a reminder of God's strength and help.

Ask parents to look at "Family Portrait" (RS-7A) from the last session to review the primary functions God intends for the family to fulfill for children. Have extra copies available for those who did not bring back their copy.

As parents, we are to provide loving nurture and an orderly, organized environment. We can seek these two things as our modest goals. To expect more of ourselves will cause us to be driven people and cause trouble in our family relationships.

❺ Good-Bye, Superparent

Objective:
To give single parents a practical way of releasing themselves from their superparent expectations (10-15 minutes).

Conclude the session with an activity that will strengthen and encourage the group members in their single parenting. Distribute a 3" x 5" index card to each parent. Ask parents to put their names on the cards. Under their names they should state one area where they are most tempted to be a superparent or where they are most likely to try compensating for the other parent.

Have parents get into pairs and exchange cards. Ask them to pray (aloud, if they are comfortable enough to do so) for the need of their partners.

Single parents need to keep in mind: the actual reality; their most important priorities; their level of energy and stress.

When they have prayed briefly for each need, have parents take a moment to write a word of encouragement on the back of the card before returning it to the owner. They may also want to exchange phone numbers for follow-up over the next weeks.

Encourage the partners to covenant to pray for each other throughout the next few weeks. Each time one is tempted in the area recorded on the card, he or she will pray for the other person in the area of their temptation. This method is effective because people can often pray with more faith for others and it guarantees that everyone is prayed for!

Close the session and prayer time by thanking God for His constant care—especially for single parents and their families.

Notes:

1. Carol Vejvoda Murdock, *Single Parents Are People, Too!* (New York: Butterick Publishing, 1980), 31.

Trust Bonds on Trial

9

Session Aim:
To explore the nature of the trust bonds between parent and child and be reassured of the strength of that bond even though it must change.

Children are born to one set of parents—a mother and a father. When there is separation from or loss of a parent, the custodial and noncustodial parents face the challenge of trust bond testing. This natural growth in children comes at a particularly difficult time for the parent because it can be very threatening to let go of one's children when you feel that you have lost so much already. The tendency is for parents to try to keep everything under their control so that no more "bad" things will happen.

It will help single parents to keep in mind the needs of their children—the need for freedom to have a loving relationship with both parents in the case of divorce or separation; the need for role models of both sexes in the case of death or desertion. It's good to remember that the children usually aren't the reason a single parent is single and must not be used as weapons in whatever conflict is going on between the parents.

Single parents need to look at their fears in this area and consciously and consistently work on ways to promote and accept the change in trust between themselves and their children.

*C*hildren usually aren't the reason a single parent is single and must not be used as weapons in conflicts between the parents.

Getting Ready

Scriptures:
Psalm 23; Luke 15:11-24.

1. Group notebook "Parenting Joys and Struggles."
2. Prepare enough copies of "Letting Trust Grow" (RS-9A), "Trust or Consequences" (RS-9B), and "Trust—The Bond That Ties" (RS-9C).

❶ Kids' View of Parents

Objective:
For single parents to think about how they may be viewed by their children (5 minutes).

Open the session by reviewing the "Parenting Joys and Struggles" notebook. Thank God for His answers to prayers and ask Him to help with each concern.

All of us have dominant personality traits or characteristics. Even our children are aware of the most obvious ones. If I were to ask your children which cartoon character you are most like, what would they say?

Give a few moments for thought and then share a personal example. If responses are slow you might mention any of the following:

- Goofy, because I'm always good for a laugh.
- Popeye, because I'm strong.
- Garfield, because I like to eat.

This is a fun way to think of how our children might see us. There are times when we feel more secure in our relationship with our children than at other times. An area that can cause insecurity is how we feel about sharing our children with the other parent, a stepparent, or a caregiver.

❷ Trust Bond Testing

Objective:
To help single parents identify anxiety they may have concerning the strength of the trust bond between them and their children (10-15 minutes).

It is good to remember that both custodial and noncustodial parents may worry that their relationship with their children will be damaged when the child spends time with the other parent or caregiver. This concern can be increased if there is also a stepparent in the picture.

Ask parents to get into groups of two to four people. Hand out copies of "Letting Trust Grow" (RS-9A), and assign a roleplay to each group. Give groups a few minutes to prepare and then take turns presenting the roleplays. Follow each roleplay with a short discussion of the problems presented and possible solutions or ways of dealings with the fears of these single parents.

Share any of the following ideas if they are not mentioned:

Children love both parents and will not always understand the reasons why they are living with one parent and not the other.

• Communication with the other parent or caregiver (in the case of the death of one parent) is always the first possible solution or way of dealing with all of the fears. Try to talk about issues such as schedules, money, discipline, communication, and value systems, either with each other or in the presence of a counselor who can help you set up guidelines for times when you and your child(ren) are together. Try to work out these things between the parents directly, not through the child.

• Always make sure fears are based on fact; not just your feelings, vain imaginations, or false reports.

• If your ex-spouse is still living and is involved in your child's life, work very hard at co-parenting. This means that parents or caregivers are working together to do what is best for the children.

• Parents must remember that children love both parents and will not always understand the reasons why they are living with one parent and not the other. Single parents must give their children the freedom to love both parents without being censored or criticized.

• Do not criticize the other parent as a person. Do discuss actions that are contrary to the Scriptures. This will help the children learn to separate sin from the sinner.

❸ What Is a Trust Bond?

Objective:
To help the single parents define and understand the origin and strength of the trust bond (10 minutes).

According to Brandt and Jackson, a trust bond "is that bond that develops between a parent and a child at the very earliest ages. Psychologists tell us that the trust bond between a parent and child begins very early—perhaps even before birth. This love relationship is essentially a molding of two individuals, the parent and child.

"Separate bonds are established between each parent and each child in the family" (37).

We can learn about the trust bond between earthly parents and children by looking at the relationship between our heavenly Father and ourselves.

Ask a volunteer to read aloud Psalm 23.

What important elements are shown in Psalm 23? (God's comfort, care, protection, availability, involvement, and nurture.)

How does God deal with our enemies? (He may not always remove them, but when we pray about them, God helps us know how to deal with them.)

Before children can succeed, they must often be allowed to fail. This is the other side of the trust bond.

How does He guide Christians through dark and dangerous places? (Through prayer, Bible reading, conversation with Christian friends, and the presence of His Holy Spirit.)

How does God comfort us when we are hurt? (He brings us healing and peace.)

As we depend on God to meet our needs, our ability to trust Him grows. Our trust bond is strengthened. It is much the same between parents and children. As an infant's needs are met by his or her parents, that child learns to depend on the parent, and trust bonds develop. The child knows that he or she can depend on the parent.

As the child grows, the bonds of trust develop a new dimension. Obviously as parents we must not keep our children dependent on us forever. Part of parental responsibility is to help our children develop independence gradually as they mature.

There is an aspect of this growing independence in children that is often hard for parents to handle. Before children can succeed, they must often be allowed to fail. This is the other side of the trust bond. Parents must trust their children enough to give them the freedom to fail. If the fall is not dangerous or the stove is not too hot, the parent will allow the child to get a bump or feel the pain if the child persists in going beyond the parent's advice.

Have someone restate the two elements of a trust bond. (1. Nurturing and protecting the young child. 2. When the child is older, the parents must have the courage to allow the child to fail.)

Point out that the trust bond is a two-way street and the growth from one element into the other should be gradual.

For what things does the child trust the parent at first? (Everything.)

What must the parents begin to do? (Slowly trust the child more and more based on his or her responsible independence.)

Have another volunteer read the familiar account of the father and his wayward son in Luke 15:11-24.

What very important aspect of the trust bond is seen in Luke 15? (The father did not reject the repentant son after his failure. He responded with unconditional love.)

This is very important for parents to remember. Failure must not be cause for rejection—whether the failure is small

f there ever was a genuine relationship with the other parent, it doesn't simply disappear and cannot be replaced."

or large. Finally, for the son or daughter to become an adult, the parents must release the child completely, even if failure seems certain—just as the father did for the prodigal son.

❹ Concept Application

Objective:
To help group members explore how these insights about the trust bond apply to the single-parent family (10-15 minutes).

Last session we talked about how we cannot be both mother and father to our children. It's just not possible.

As Brandt and Jackson point out, "If there ever was a genuine relationship with the other parent, it doesn't simply disappear and cannot be replaced. If this fact is ignored, serious emotional consequences can result.

"The other side of this principle is the fact that the influence of the other parent cannot seriously threaten or replace the trust bond you have with your child. However, that doesn't mean your children won't try to manipulate you by comparing you or playing you against their other parent or caregiver. Such attempts are normal. There is also the problem of a parent or caregiver constantly criticizing the other. This can color the child's perspective and may need to be talked about in your co-parenting situation with or without help of a counselor. If your ex-spouse refuses to discuss these issues, it may be necessary to get a mediator" (37-38).

Name three important aspects of a trust bond.

(1. Once established, it is not easily threatened by external influences.

2. Separate bonds are established between each parent and each child in the family.

3. As children mature, the trust bond must adjust to release the children, allowing them to experience ever-increasing levels of responsibility for their own lives.)

Have parents get into groups of four people. Give each person a copy of "Trust or Consequences" (RS-9B), and have the parents work on it together, discussing why they think one response is better than another or making suggestions they think will work better.

After five to eight minutes have the large group reconvene to discuss their answers. Point out that in real life, responses will be based on many variables. There may or may not be an absolutely right answer, and that's why room is provided for parents to offer suggestions in areas where they have had

t is often easier to see what others should do than to recognize what we should do personally.

experience. Here are some suggestions with explanation:

1. C is preferred although it might not hurt to talk with Miguel's father first. You can offer Miguel some help on how to work it out with his father. Miguel could tell his father how much he likes to be with him and ask him to call when he's going to be late or cannot make it.
2. C is preferred. Children need our help in working out problems even of their own making, just as we do. A variation of D would also be helpful. Rather than blaming Joanie, her father could help her devise a plan for replacing her bike.
3. B is preferred, along with C and A. Bedtime ritual helps young children feel secure. This is the time that children will often talk about what's bothering them. Once the activity of the day stops, little ones may begin to feel their emotions more.
4. C is preferred. Consistency and security are important here. Mom should also make sure that Robert is eating enough at meal times. If he is in day-care she should check with the caregiver.
5. B is preferred. Providing supervision besides a parent will help Timmy gain some independence appropriate to his age.

❺ What about Tomorrow?

Objective:
To help the single parents identify the next step in exercising the trust bond with each of their children (10-15 minutes).

It is often easier to see what others should do than to recognize what we should do personally. Let's move from the laboratory into real life.

With the group together, hand out copies of "Trust—The Bond That Ties" (RS-9C).

Ask parents to complete this worksheet for each child. Have them identify one area of trust for each child before filling in the last two columns. Encourage parents to talk with each other and you to get ideas about what they might do next.

After several minutes, close in prayer, asking that the Lord will give the parents wisdom as they try to take the appropriate next steps of trust.

Independent and Responsible

10

To help group members model independent dependence on God.

Those who work with single parents say it normally takes about two to three years for the single parent to get his or her life back to a semblance of order following divorce or death. In order for single parents to teach children how to be independent and responsible people, they need to have taken steps in this area as well.

Children spend much time balancing their conflicting feelings about growing up. They want to be grown-up and independent yet still enjoy childish privileges of dependency and limited responsibilities. Most children want to make right decisions and keep their word. But, it is easy for them to forget or seem to forget.

Single parents need the help that their children can give for survival as a single parent family. Experts agree that children are much more able to handle responsibilities than parents might expect. Again, you might ask each parent to tell one responsibility they have given each of their children that not only helps to get the work done but helps teach children how to be responsible and independent.

Single parents can be good examples of independence and responsibility. They can best teach their children these qualities by demonstrating independent, responsible behavior themselves.

Single parents need the help that their children can give them for survival as single parents.

Getting Ready

Scriptures:
Psalm 20:7, 8; Psalm 37:5;
Proverbs 3:5, 6.

1. Group notebook "Parenting Joys and Struggles."
2. Prepare enough copies of "Just Checking" (RS-10A), "How Do Your Children Grow?" (RS-10B—two sheets), and "Next Steps" (RS-10C—parents will need one copy per child).

❶ What Does It Mean to Be Mature?

Objective:
To have single parents discuss the meaning of maturity (5-10 minutes).

Ask parents as they come into the session if they would like to add requests or answers to the "Parenting Joys and Struggles" notebook. Pray short sentence prayers with anyone who enters a request or answer.

- **When you were eight years old what did you want to be when you grew up?**
- **What do you hear your children say they want to be when they are grown up?**

Allow a few minutes for parents to respond.

Hopes and dreams for the future are very important. Motivational speaker and consultant Joel Barker says that children who have a goal for their future vocation do better in school and are better adjusted than those who do not have hope.

Dreaming attainable dreams and setting realistic goals are part of the journey to maturity. Maturity is an interesting concept to contemplate.

Within the Christian context, when we say someone is mature, what do we mean? (A mature person is independent and able to manage most of the basic tasks of day-to-day living, make responsible decisions, hold a job, earn a living, accomplish domestic tasks, handle emotions in a healthy way, initiate and sustain intimate relationships, handle his or her sexuality according to biblical standards, and actively serve Christ. Being able to function independently does not mean we do not need other people. The whole model of the Body of Christ in the Bible is one of interdependence. However, the mature person is independent in that he or she can give as well as receive.)

This is quite a list. Parents have a big responsibility in training their children to be mature. This is difficult in a two-parent family and can be overwhelming in a single-parent family. The first step in this process is to see how we are doing as parents.

**F**unctioning independently does not mean we don't need other people. The model of the body of Christ is one of interdependence.

❷ My Maturity Gauge

Objective:
To help single parents rate their own maturity level (5-10 minutes).

Hand out copies of "Just Checking" (RS-10A). Ask parents to work independently, assuring them that this is not a test and no one else will see it. Have the group members identify the category or area with the lowest scores. Encourage them to jot down some realistic ideas for improving this area during the next three to six months. Suggest that they keep the sheet to look at in several months to see how they have grown.

If time allows, have volunteers ask questions or make comments.

❸ Our Goal— Independently Dependent on God

Objective:
To help parents recognize or reaffirm that the ability to be independent has a solid foundation if they are dependent on God (10 minutes).

Before we talk about how we can help our children in this area, we need to look at God's Word.

List the following Scripture references on the chalk or marker board. Have parents identify the key word in each passage and define it.

Psalm 20:7, 8—*(Trust)*
Psalm 37:5—*(Commit/trust)*
Proverbs 3:5, 6—*(Trust)*

God wants to be involved in each area of our lives. He is able to help us grow in areas where we are weak. Look back at "Just Checking" (RS-10A). Ask God to show you one area where you can grow and increase your dependence on Him. Put a star by that skill.

❹ How Does My Child Grow?

Objective:
To help single parents evaluate the level of their children's independence and plan one specific strategy for helping each child develop independence and responsibility (20-25 minutes).

We've been looking at our own development; now let's consider some of the growing-up or developmental tasks that children need to master.

Hand out copies of "How Does Your Child Grow?" (RS-10B). Group parents according to the age of their *oldest* child. If your group is large enough, form a small group for each of the five stages listed—infant, toddler, preschool, elementary, and adolescent. If your group is small, use two groups—infant through preschool and elementary through adolescent.

Write the name of your oldest child still at home in the appropriate place on the sheet. As a group, read the list of tasks. Check each task that your child has already mastered.

Have the parents stay in the same small groups as they will

be doing another activity together.

Allow group members to ask questions or share any new insights they may have received as a result of this activity.

After a few minutes of discussion, distribute enough copies of "Next Steps" (RS-10C) so that each parent has one for each of his or her children.

Ask parents to follow along as you talk them through an example:

Fill in your child's name and indicate the developmental stage that the child is in—infant, toddler, preschool, etc. Then look at your resource sheet, "How Do Your Children Grow?" (RS-10B) to identify any tasks your child still needs to master in this stage and write down under number three on "Next Steps" (RS-10C). Put a star by tasks that your child is ready to conquer. For example, maybe elementary-age Bobby has trouble saving any of his money for special purchases.

Under number four select one task listed in number three that you would like to help your child work on right away. For number five, have your group brainstorm ways to help your child. Maybe for Bobby, it would be to get him to keep an accurate record of how he spends his money. (Before he can control his money, he must know what is happening to it.)

Number six asks you to identify what you must do to get the growth under way. Maybe Bobby's mom or dad need to get Bobby a little note pad and show him how to keep an account. They could check how he is doing when they give him his weekly allowance.

Encourage parents to take the sheets home and complete one for each of their children.

Show a sample of the chart below on newsprint or the board and suggest the following idea to the group:

Preschool Responsibilities:	Sun.	Mon.	Tues.	Wed.	Thurs.	Fri.	Sat.
Picking up toys							
Being kind							
Brushing teeth							
Washing hands							

You might make a simple responsibility chart for each child with a list of duties appropriate to his or her

Try a simple responsibility chart for each child with a list of duties appropriate to his or her age.

age. Make up the charts using "How Does Your Child Grow?" (RS-10B) as a guideline. The child can check off his/her duties each day as they are completed. This will give you and your child a guide for their progress in independence and responsibility.

For older children, you might want to include weekly jobs—things that they are responsible to do for an entire week. This might include emptying the trash, keeping the bathroom clean, or feeding the dog (or cat, or fish, or ?). As your children get older, you may want to tie their allowance to the completion of their jobs.

❺ Trust Prayers

Objective:
To have single parents seek God's guidance as they help their children to become independently dependent on Him (5-10 minutes).

Have people think back to the Scripture passages (Psalms 20:7, 8; 37:5, and Proverbs 3:5, 6) and ask them to put one passage into their own words as a prayer. They should write this prayer at the bottom of RS-10C.

Close the session by having volunteers read their prayers to the group.

Self-Esteem and Sexual Identity

11

Session Aim:
To increase single parents' understanding of the importance of sexual identity in the development of their children's self-esteem.

Single parents often wonder what impact growing up in a one-parent home will have on their children. They ask questions like:

• "How will Jason learn to be a man, if he lives with just his sister and me?"

• "How can Julia and Megan understand what a relationship between a husband and wife is like if their dad is no longer in our home?"

These are natural questions. Single parents want their children to be adjusted well to their own sexuality, and they want them to know how to get along with the opposite sex. It is usually expected that these tasks be accomplished in the home as children interact with two parents—a role model of each sex.

A child's sexual identity has its roots in self-esteem. Single parents need to realize that they play an important part in building their child's sense of self-esteem and must provide ways to meet their child's needs for interaction with members of the opposite sex. This is generally more difficult for women to do than for men because there are usually more female caregivers and teachers—especially in the lower grades. Whether male or female, single parents need to consciously plan for healthy role models of both sexes for their children.

Single parents want their children to adjust well to their own sexuality and know how to get along with the opposite sex.

Getting Ready

Scriptures:
Genesis 1:27; 2:7, 22; Proverbs 31:29; Isaiah 32:8; Genesis 3:16; Exodus 35:22; Isaiah 38:19; Luke 8:1-3; Acts 4:32; Joshua 1:14; Ezra 10:1; I Corinthians 11:11; Ephesians 5:21, 25, 33; Numbers 18:7; Acts 5:14.

1. Group notebook "Parenting Joys and Struggles."
2. Prepare enough copies of "Created in His Image" (RS-11A), "So What's The Difference?" (RS-11B), "Three Components of Self-Esteem" (RS-11C), "What I Can Do Best" (RS-11D).

---

❶ Fun with Stereotypes

Objective:
For single parents to reflect on how our society views men and women (5 to 10 minutes).

Review the requests and answers in the "Parenting Joys and Struggles" notebook. Encourage parents to add their concerns and answers. Plan to include them in your closing prayer.

On the board or newsprint write the following titles as column headings:

Real Men Don't Eat Quiche   Real Women Don't Pump Gas

Several years ago there were books that spoofed stereotyped sex roles. You might remember *Real Men Don't Eat Quiche* and *Real Women Don't Pump Gas*. Let's take a few minutes to come up with a list of current-day stereotypes about men and women. Tell me any stereotypes you are aware of—whether you believe them or not!

Quickly go around the room and have each person give you one stereotype for men and one for women. If ideas are still flowing, go around the group a second time. Let your group have fun with this activity.

We haven't established what men and women should or should not do. But we have shown that some of the differences between men and women are culturally based.

Before we go further, we need to see what the Bible tells us about sexual identity.

---

❷ In His Image

Objective:
To help single parents discover how God views men and women and study some instances of sexual identity in the Bible (10-15 minutes).

Ask someone to read Genesis 1:27, and take a few minutes to discuss the meaning of the verse.

What does being created in the image of God mean as far as differences between men and women? (People as a whole have many qualities and abilities which are alike for men and women in reflecting our Creator. Being created in

B
oth men and women have a likeness to God that affects how they relate to others—how they love, show feelings, express concern.

His image means that all people share, though imperfectly, something of God's nature. Both men and women have a likeness to God that affects how they relate to others—how they love, show feelings, express concern. Even though both male and female sinned at the Fall, God's mark may be seen in both sexes.)

Ask parents to get into two groups. Hand out copies of "Created in His Image" (RS-11A). Explain that each group is to look up the assigned verses and write an acrostic to form the words "Men" and "Women" that reflects the similarities and differences between them as given in the Scriptures. Note that the selected verses are only a partial list of many examples of the roles, functions, and attributes of men and women. The purpose of this activity is to help the group members see some of the ways that men and women are alike and different.

After five to ten minutes, bring the groups together and have them read their findings aloud. Finished acrostics might look something like these:

Group I:
Man was made from the dust (Gen. 2:7)—different
Eve was made from Adam's rib (Gen. 2:22)—different
Noble deeds are done by men and women (Prov. 31:29, Isa. 32:8)—alike

Women alone can give birth (Gen. 3:16)—different
Offerings were given by men and women (Exod. 35:22)—alike
Men can be fathers (Isa. 38:19)—different
Even women travelled with Jesus (Luke 8:1-3)—alike
No one claimed possessions were his or her own (Acts 4:32)—alike

Group II:
Men were to fight for land; women stayed home (Josh. 1:14)—different
Everyone—men, women, and children—wept and confessed sin (Ezra 10:1)—alike
Neither men nor women are independent of each other (I Cor. 11:11)—alike

Women and men are to be submitted to each other in the Lord (Eph. 5:21)—alike
Only (Levite) men were priests (Num. 18:7)—different

*S*ome differences between men and women are biological, others are cultural, and others—though not biological—are still God-ordained.

Men are to love their wives as Christ loved the Church (Eph. 5:25)—different

Even when they disagree, a wife can respect her husband (Eph. 5:33)—different

Need to believe in the Lord (Acts 5:14)—alike

Some of these differences are biological, others are cultural, and others—though not biological—are still God-ordained. Children in single-parent families need to have close relationships with married couples to see the biblical model of marriage lived out. This is where the church and extended family can play an important role.

❸ Vive la Difference!

Objective:
To help single parents understand and appreciate some of the differences between males and females. (10 minutes).

Let's take another look at differences between men and women (5-10 minutes). Hand out copies of "So What's the Difference?" (RS-11B).

Have volunteers read through the chart—first a male characteristic and then a corresponding female characteristic. Point out that there aren't many differences in terms of what males and females can do distinct from each other. Insert comments and explanations as indicated below.

- Men can be fathers.
- Women can be mothers.
- Because males have larger muscles, slight differences in bone structure, and a better oxygen delivery system, they tend to be stronger, faster, and more agile.
- Women tend to excel in certain endurance tests because they are more flexible. They seem to have tolerance for pain and develop earlier, both physically and mentally.

This may have an effect on education and be the reason that boys and girls seem to excel in different subjects. Those subjects may be taught when the mind of one sex is more receptive than the other.

- Males are more susceptible to some physical and emotional diseases.
- Women seem to have more problems with depression.
- More females are born, and they live longer.

*W*hen discussing male and female differences, we need to distinguish between variations that are due to culture and those that are due to gender.

Other apparent differences may not be due to gender, but to personality. However, some tests suggest specific male or female tendencies.

• In general, males are more spatially oriented and aggressive.

• Females are usually more intuitive and more verbal.

When discussing male and female differences, we need to be careful to distinguish between variations that are due to culture rather than gender.

In many ways, it seems like it was easier in Bible times than now to teach children about their maleness or femaleness. Children grew up surrounded by a large family, extended family, and servants. In terms of occupation, there were also fewer options open to either men or women. Today, one of the main concerns of single parents is that their children do not have models of the opposite sex to help them adjust to their own sexuality and to teach them how to get along with the opposite sex.

To understand how to deal with this concern, we must first look at the roots of a child's overall self-esteem.

❹ Sexual Identity Development

Objective:
To help parents understand the development of sexual identity in the context of self-esteem and how they contribute to the development of their child's sexual identity (10-15 minutes).

Hand out copies of "Three Components of Self-Esteem" (RS-11C). Tell parents to visualize self-esteem as a three-legged stool, and ask them to label the legs "sense of worth," "sense of adequacy," and "sense of identity" (Brandt and Jackson, 44).

What happens when one leg of a stool is missing? (It tips over.)

What happens when one leg is too long or too short? (The stool is not stable.)

Just as we need all three legs of a stool to be secure and equal, so children need to have a strong sense of worth, adequacy, and identity.

The sense-of-worth leg represents a child's feeling of being loved, and parents are the most significant persons in communicating this to a child. At any early age, children can begin to understand that they are worth enough to God that His Son died for them. A child's

T
he parent of the same sex as the child has the most to contribute to the child's feelings of competence.

sense of being loved by his or her heavenly and earthly parents is very essential to the child's well-being.

Love includes several things which can all be adequately provided by the single parent. What are some of those things? (Statements like, "I love you"; warm hugs and kisses; affectionate touches; special remembrances; cheerful provision of necessities; fair discipline; celebration of success.)

A sense of adequacy is the feeling of competence—the confidence that "I can do it." This is developed in children as they explore the world and develop new skills.

Most marriage and family counselors agree that the parent of the same sex as the child has the most to contribute to these feelings of competence.

The sense of identity is the child's certainty that he or she belongs and is unique—being a part of the family and yet being especially unique. These two aspects of identity must be balanced.

How can a parent help to create a sense of belonging for everyone in the family? (Planning "together" activities, using inclusive words such as "we," establishing family traditions, doing shared chores, and making shared decisions.)

In what ways can a child's uniqueness and specialness be fostered? (By valuing what each child can contribute. Each child can develop a specialty. Be careful not to compare children negatively to siblings with comments such as, "Why don't you keep your room clean like Margo?" or "Jose could ride his two-wheeler before he started kindergarten!")

The "identity" leg of the stool includes a child's sexual identity—the confidence within the child concerning his or her own gender and an understanding of what that means behaviorally. At a young age a child should learn his or her gender with certainty. This important process needs stable and consistent contacts with adults of both sexes.

Have volunteers read aloud the material on "Three Components of Self-Esteem." Allow a few minutes for comments or questions before having the group members fill in the summary chart at the bottom of the resource sheet. When completed, the chart should look like this:

The parent of the opposite sex as the child has the most to contribute to the child's sense of being sexually different from that parent.

WHAT EACH PARENT PROVIDES BEST

	Mother	Father
Sons	"I am loved." Affirms male identity.	"I am loved." "I can do it." Provides role model.
Daughters	"I am loved." "I can do it." Provides role model.	"I am loved." Affirms female identity.

❺ Enhancing Sexual Identity

Objective:
To help single parents identify ways they can best help each of their children establish a healthy sexual identity (15-20 minutes).

Have the group divide into smaller groups of three people each. Encourage people who know each other well to group together. Hand out copies of "What I Can Do Best" (RS-11D). Have parents fill in the blanks in the center two columns by using complete sentences containing their child's name in the following fashion: "In terms of sexual identity, I can help Johnny . . ." and "A person of the opposite sex is needed to help Johnny. . . ."

Then in the right-hand column have parents list the names of two or three people of the appropriate sex who might be able to help. Possible candidates are the noncustodial parent, grandparents, aunts and uncles, scout leaders, persons in Big Brother/Big Sister or other club programs, Sunday school teachers, concerned church members, and caring neighbors.

Direct the group's attention to the tips at the bottom of RS-11D.

Now that you have some suggestions for who might help your family in terms of sexual-identity balance, you will want to put the plan into practice. There are several cautions to keep in mind.

Don't be tempted to think that your children will be adequately exposed to adults of the opposite sex as they naturally move into the broader community. Children of a single-parent father may not have any problem being exposed to women, but according to authors Patricia Brandt and Dave Jackson, women with children who need to interact with men have less than one chance in ten of having a male teacher in the average school or Sunday school (46).

You need to be deliberate about planning. Here's how:

**C**hildren who need to interact with men have a less than one chance in ten of having a male teacher in the school or Sunday school.

1. When you approach people to help, tell them why you want to involve other adults in the lives of your children. Use notes from this session.

2. Use caution in deciding who to ask. If you have any reservations about the trustworthiness of the person, trust your intuition, and find someone else. Based on statistics on child abuse, relatives, baby-sitters, and family acquaintances are not necessarily safe.

3. If you are dating, it is probably unwise to expect the person you are dating to fulfill these identity needs for your children. Such expectations could load the relationship with too much baggage, and it might be too unstable for your children. If you have a commitment to marriage, your future spouse can meet some of your children's needs. Even so, it is a good idea to keep other adults involved with your children.

4. Be careful to not let the arrangement with a helping adult involve you emotionally in a way with which you are not comfortable. The close working relationship may cause you and the other person to feel like you are parenting together. Take care that the relationship does not become physically involved or adulterous. Some safeguards:

- Involve another person
- Work together in a larger group
- Involve the noncustodial parent as much as possible
- Seek help from close relatives

By keeping these precautions in mind, you can successfully find other adults to help your children grow in the area of self-esteem and sexual identity.

Close the session in prayer, asking the Lord to help the parents as they seek assistance in areas where they need it. Be sure to include any requests from the prayer and praise notebook.

Picking Up Our Social Stitches

12

Session Aim:
To help single parents explore new social and emotional outlets and handle their uneasiness about building a new social life.

Carol Vejvoda Murdock writes to single parents, "The worst thing that can happen to you as a single parent is to fall out of the social web that supports us all. We're humans, highly social beings, so we arrive in the world already knit into an intricate pattern of relationships . . . family, friends, neighbors, the community, then families of our own. . . . Now, as a single parent, you've a dropped stitch in this warm, comforting shawl of humanity. One of the linking threads is broken. And you can slowly ravel right out of the pattern unless you make a conscious effort to knit yourself back in."[1]

The writer suggests that single parents need to start repairing their lifeline as soon as they can. She says, "Your emotional well-being—and your children's—depends on it."

Single parents need to guard against trying to make their children fill the void created by the loss or absence of a spouse. As we have seen in earlier sessions, single parents also must not try to compensate for the lack of two parents in their children's lives. They can start reaching out to other parents, grandparents, other relatives, friends, and perhaps moving into support groups in the church or community where new friendships can be made.

Guard against trying to make your children fill the void created by the loss or absence of your spouse.

Getting Ready

Scriptures:
I Corinthians 6:13b, 18-20;
I Corinthians 10:13, 14.

1. To enhance the atmosphere of fun and social contact, prepare or have someone else prepare coffee, tea, and light snacks to be served before the session.
2. Write the following questions on chalkboard or newsprint: Since being a single parent:

   • What was your best family adventure?
   • What was your best adult adventure?
   • What new adventure would you like to try?
   • What's stopping you?

3. Prepare enough copies of "Have You Tried This Adventure?" (RS-12A), "Picking Up Dropped Stitches" (RS-12B), and "Why Do I Feel This Way?" (RS-12C—optional).
4. Blank sheets of paper for Step 5.

❶ Repair Work Ahead!

Objective:
To help single parents explore where they feel they fit socially in the world around them (5 minutes).

As people come in, invite them to enjoy the refreshments and visit for a few minutes. Then ask them to be seated and begin with prayer, thanking God for each of them.

Read aloud the quoted material in the introduction this session, and ask parents to discuss what the author has said. To get the discussion going, you might ask:

What has your experience been in the area of having your social needs met? While being sensitive to those who feel they have been overlooked or left out socially, be careful not to let this session turn into a gripe session. You want real feelings expressed, but keep the focus on what each person can do to get involved in healthy social outlets.

In this session, we're going to look at ways to "knit yourself back in(to). . . the warm, comforting shawl of humanity."

❷ Adventures Ahead

Objective:
To help single parents discover new social activities for the entire family, as well as for themselves with other adults (10-15 minutes).

Give everyone a sheet of paper and pencil or pen. Ask parents to write down their answers to the questions on the chalkboard or newsprint. Talk the parents through the questions as follows so that they can make their answers more specific:

• **What was your best family adventure? Answer this question in terms of your single-parent family. What** activity or outing has been most enjoyable for you and all your children?

- What was your best adult adventure? Again the time frame is since you have been a single parent. It doesn't have to be some great exploit—just what's been most enjoyable to you.
- What new adventure would you like to try? Answer this in two parts: as a family and as an adult apart from your children. Don't list things that are financially unreasonable for you, but do list what you'd like to do if other hurdles could be overcome.
- What's stopping you? Answer this in two parts also: for the family and for yourself alone.

Allow the group about five minutes to answer these questions.

After the group members have jotted down their answers, hand out copies of "Have You Tried This Adventure?" (RS-12A). Have as many parents as possible tell their answers to the questions.

Encourage listeners to mark any ideas they hear that are on the list and that they might like to try or to write down ones that are not on the list that they would like to try. The purpose is to help the single parents broaden their horizons concerning adventures that they—as families or individuals—can do. Suggest that if they want to do something which someone else has done with their family, to write the person's name next to the activity as a good resource for information and encouragement in overcoming any hurdles they see.

Single parents may fall into the common trap of thinking that all their difficulties—social, emotional, etc.—are a result of their singleness. This can lead to the "Poor Me" syndrome in which parents think others are avoiding them or leaving them out. Help them recognize that every adult must deal with feelings of exclusion. The truth is, there are far more people who are waiting to respond to an invitation than to extend one. Whether single or married, the people with the most satisfying social lives are ones who reach out instead of waiting for someone else to initiate. Throughout this session listen for "Poor Me" comments ("No one ever sits with me in church," or "You don't get invited over to other people's homes unless you're a couple too."). While such comments may be valid,

S ingles cannot change everyone around them, but they can change themselves.

singles cannot change everyone around them. They can change themselves. This would be a good opportunity to help singles think in terms of making things happen, rather than watching or waiting for them to happen.

❸ Outward Bound With the Kids

Objective:
To help single parents find some possible solutions for overcoming difficult challenges of finding social outlets for their families (10-15 minutes).

"One of life's hardest tasks is that of deciding to risk. Failure is a very real possibility in every new adventure. But it is well to remember that it is in the possibility of failure that the joy of success is born" (48).

Distribute copies of "Picking Up Dropped Stitches," (RS-12B) and read over the list of situations in Part I. Have the parents get into groups of two or three and assign one or more situations to each small group. Allow about five minutes for the small groups to discuss their assigned scenario and the related risks and possible solutions.

As a large group again, discuss each situation, the suggested risks, and possible solutions. If any of the possible responses listed below are not mentioned by the single parents, bring them up yourself.

SITUATION 1: Going camping for the first time with your three grade-school-age children.
Risk: Little experience in putting up a tent; may be surrounded by people you don't know or no people at all; getting lost; how to handle meals and everything else by yourself.
Solution: Camp with another family who has camping experience; start with just an overnight; ask someone to help you with the tent; rent a camper; plan simple, easy-to-prepare meals and cook some things ahead of time.

SITUATION 2: Going to a family reunion for the first time without a spouse.
Risk: How to deal with spoken and unspoken questions; feeling comfortable with all the couples.
Solution: Share some of your concerns with a close relative who can "run interference" for you; plan some activities or conversation starters; invite a close friend to go with you.

SITUATION 3: Your nine-year-old son begs you to take him to a football game. You've never been to one, and you are sure you won't like it.

Risk: Feeling lonely in a crowd of enthusiastic sports fans; not knowing how to act; not understanding the rules of the game.
Solution: Watch a few games on television to practice; ask a friend to explain the parts of the game and the calls that you don't understand; consider having one your son's friends and his mom (or dad) go with you; decide that you will enjoy it if your son is having fun.

SITUATION 4: Attending church family functions such as picnics, potlucks, family camp, etc. without a spouse.
Risk: Not finding someone friendly to sit with; talking to people you haven't met; keeping track of the children and making them obey.
Solution: Find out who else is planning on attending and plan to sit together; look for someone else who looks lonely and introduce yourself; invite a friend to go with you; for family camp ask a teenager from church to help you with the children.

SITUATION 5: Taking children shopping (particularly for men).
Risk: Not finding what's needed; children want to browse and you want to buy what you came after and leave; losing the children.
Solution: Set a time limit; if the children are old enough, let them "pre-shop" alone and then you join them to make the decisions and write the checks; plan with the children what to do if you get separated.

SITUATION 6: Giving a sleep-over birthday party for one of the children.
Risk: You might lose control of kids and your house will be damaged; someone could get hurt; no sleep.
Solution: Ask a responsible teenager or college student to help with some active games; plan enough activities to get the kids tired; limit the number of guests; avoid serving food that is loaded with sugar; plan to take a nap or go to bed early the next day.

Single parents struggle to handle their need for emotional and physical closeness without compromising God's standards.

❹ Outward Bound With Adults

Objective:
To help single parents find healthy, biblical ways of handling concerns about their social life and need for emotional intimacy (15-20 minutes).

Direct the parents' attention to Part II of "Picking Up Dropped Stitches" (RS-12B). Discuss each social situation and its challenges as you did for the situations with children. If you have a lively and close-knit group, have volunteers roleplay each situation.

SITUATION 1: You've decided it is time to get involved at church and to meet some new friends. The adult Single Parents' Group has a hayride and cookout planned for two weeks from tomorrow.
Risk: Feeling awkward with a group of new people; not fitting in with the rest of the group.
Solution: Always go with a friend—if possible, one who has been to the group before and can introduce you to people; if this particular activity does not appeal to you, wait for one that does.

SITUATION 2: Mutual friends have had you and another single over for an evening of dinner and games. You find this person very attractive and sense that he (she) feels the same way about you. He (she) invites you and the same friends for dinner. After the friends leave . . . .
Risk: Getting emotionally involved before you really know each other; being tempted to get physically involved.
Solution: Determine to take this relationship (and any other) slowly; be ready to leave when your friends do, but suggest that you get together again.

SITUATION 3: You want to go on the weekend retreat with your small group from church, but everyone else in the group is married.
Risk: You may feel left out if the activities are couple-oriented.
Solution: Find out from the retreat leader whether the topic and activities will be sensitive to singles; ask if you could invite a close friend to attend.

SITUATION 4: Two single parents have been dating each other for a year. One of them is eager to marry and the other isn't.
Risk: Hurt feelings; the person who is not eager for marriage may feel pressured into it.
Solution: Discuss whether or not the relationship can continue as a friendship; stop seeing each other for an agreed-upon amount of time; both begin seeing other people.

Give parents the opportunity to suggest and discuss other social situations that are a challenge to singles.

NOTE: The following material on physical intimacy is optional. Based on the composition of your group and your comfort level with this topic, decide what is best for your group. It is recommended that all group members receive a copy of "Why Do I Feel This Way?" (RS-12C) for at-home use.

A very real challenge for single parents is how to handle their need for emotional intimacy and physical closeness with other adults without compromising God's standards. This is especially difficult because single parents (except those who are parents due to adoption) have already experienced the fulfillment of a sexual relationship. There is much wrong thinking in this area among Christians. God's Word makes it very clear that He expects pure moral behavior.

Hand out "Why Do I Feel This Way?" (RS-12C), and have parents read it silently. Use your own judgment to decide how much group discussion is needed.

Ask the parents to find I Corinthians 6:13b, 18-20 in their Bibles. Read the passage aloud. You might ask others who have different versions of the Bible to read this passage aloud, too.

Ask parents to write the passage in their own words. (They can use the back of a resource sheet.) After a minute or two ask several to read what they have written. Example: Sexual sin damages my closeness to God. Point out that God created sexual intimacy as part of His plan for married couples. Just as wild flowers are beautiful and last only in the context for which they were created, physical intimacy is beautiful in marriage.

Ask someone to find and read I Corinthians 10:13, 14. Say that this is a promise of God that single parents can count on in the area of sexual feelings that are difficult to handle. Verse 14 makes it clear how to handle these temptations—Flee! This verse, along with some of the suggestions in "Why Do I Feel This Way?" (RS-12C), will help them if they are honestly and sincerely seeking help.

Too often Christians plan a romantic evening with an atmosphere of intimacy and then wonder how things got out of hand. Part of fleeing is not even setting the stage for action. One single mom had this wise attitude, "I never wanted to start something that I was not free to finish."

B ut when you are tempted, [God] will also provide a way out."

Give parents a few minutes for the opportunity to write a contract with God concerning this important and sensitive area of their life. A contract is an agreement to do something—agree with God how you will handle your sexual feelings. Suggest that parents keep the contract in their Bibles marking the promise passage of I Corinthians 10:13, 14.

❺ Moving On Out

Objective:
To help single parents plan a new social strategy which addresses both activity and intimacy needs (5 minutes).

Give each person a blank sheet of paper to use in planning his or her "perfect day." Have parents team up with a partner and talk together about what new adventure each person would like to do. Have them select from that day one activity that is possible and plan how it can be carried out.

Suggest that team members agree to contact one another at least once during the week—either in person or by phone. The time together should be spent in mutual accountability concerning whether any progress has been made on carrying out their new plan for adventure.

Have the "Parenting Joys and Struggles" notebook available for your closing prayer time. Ask parents to tell requests and report answers. Close with sentence prayers for each request in the notebook that has not been answered and those mentioned. Remember to thank God for answered prayers and for His great and all-encompassing love for us.

Notes:

1. Carol Vejvoda Murdock, *Single Parents Are People, Too!* (New York: Butterick Publishing, 1980), 91.

Extended Family– Successful Family

13

Session Aim:
To help single parents utilize the resources of the extended family, the church family, and friends.

We were left on this earth in a body to be there for one another, to help and build one another up. . . . Don't try to be an island. We are social by nature. Get a friend or relative to help you with certain matters, get advice from experts. . . . Just because you are without a spouse doesn't mean you don't need people in your life. Be a friend. Look for and ask God for people to fill your life with love and support. That is one of the most important ingredients for a successfully single life. . . ."[1]

"Do not be afraid; you will not suffer shame.
Do not fear disgrace; you will not be humiliated.
You will forget the shame of your youth and remember no more the reproach of your widowhood.
For your Maker is your husband—
The Lord Almighty is his name—
    the Holy One of Israel is your Redeemer;
    he is called the God of all the earth.
The Lord will call you back as if you were a wife
    deserted and distressed in spirit—
a wife who married young, only to be rejected," says
    your God.
"For a brief moment I abandoned you, but with deep
    compassion I will bring you back."

—Isaiah 54:4-7

*J*ust because you are without a spouse doesn't mean you don't need people in your life."

Getting Ready

Scriptures:
I John 4:11-13; Psalms 27:14; 55:22; 71:20; 146:9; Jeremiah 29:11; Nahum 1:7; Matthew 11:28; II Corinthians 1:5; 4:17; Ephesians 4:25-32.

1. The group notebook "Parenting Joys and Struggles."
2. Prepare enough copies of "Help! Case Studies" (RS-13A), "Heavenly Help" (RS-13B), "Family Unity" (RS-13C), and "Helping Hands Exchange" (RS-13D).
3. Optional: copies of the Bibliography.
4. A package of 3" x 5" index cards to be used in Steps 1 and 4.
5. A bulletin board with tacks or stickpins or a posterboard or wall to which you can safely tape cards.
6. Books listed in the Bibliography from the church library. You might invite the church librarian to be present.
7. Refreshments to conclude the session and the course. You might ask another group in the church (Sunday school class, deacons, etc.) to provide and serve to show their interest and care.

❶ Prayer Works

Objective:
To provide the group members an opportunity to develop a prayer network (10-15 minutes).

Ask parents to tell one way they have been helped as a result of the course in *Parenting Alone*—one thing they learned, tried, felt encouraged about, etc. Affirm each person who shares and thank God for the progress that has been made. Encourage parents to continue to work in the areas that God has brought to their attention through your time together.

When the group members are done sharing, direct attention to the group notebook, "Parenting Joys and Struggles." Review the needs which are indicated in the notebook or have been added throughout the sessions.

Encourage parents to continue to pray for each other by using one of the following options:

1. Have 3" x 5" index cards with each parent's name and phone number written on them (one parent to a card). Ask parents to each take one card and continue to contact and pray for that person for an agreed-upon period of time such as three months. They can decide if they want to continue at the end of that time.

2. Ask parents to get in groups of two. Have them write their name and phone number on a 3" x 5" index card and exchange them to be prayer partners for up to three months or longer.

3. Ask parents who would like a prayer partner to fill out a 3" x 5" card index with their name and phone number. Tell them you will give their card to a member in church who will

**A** single dad could form a *"family"* with another single dad and his children to share the expenses and work load.

be contacting them to be a prayer partner for a specific period of time.

Review the answers to prayer. Then spend some time in conversational prayer, praising and thanking God for the answers and asking for His help with the concerns parents continue to have.

❷ The Kin Connection

Objective:
To help single parents understand the importance of the extended family in meeting emotional, social, physical, and spiritual needs in the single-parent family (10-15 minutes).

Hand out copies of the resource sheet, "Help! Case Studies" (RS-13A) and ask parents to get into groups of two or three. Assign one case study to each group—you don't have to do all of them.

Ask each group to analyze their case and answer the following questions you have written on a chalk or marker board.

- **What is happening in this family?**
- **What emotional, physical, social, and/or spiritual needs are present?**
- **How might the need be met or eased by other people in the immediate or extended family—including church family?**

Allow about ten minutes for small group discussion and suggestions before asking each small group to report their case and conclusions to the whole class.

If not mentioned by the group members, make the following suggestions for how the needs of each single family could be met:

Zack: Could form a "family" with another single dad and his children to share the expenses and work load; an at-home mom could provide child care as a ministry or at a reduced rate.

Steven: Mom could ask a trustworthy man from church or older male relative to spend regular time with Steven; she could talk to Douglas about his difficulty in relating to his brother; she could seek family counseling; she could enlist the help of a male youth worker.

Joanne: Could talk with the pastor or other church to get the name of a Christian teacher who could tutor Ryan and give practical helps to Joanne; she could have a responsible teen from church or a male relative help tutor Ryan; she

 **single mom could ask a trustworthy man from church or older male relative to spend regular time with her son.**

could request that the school test Ryan for learning disabilies; if any are present, she could locate and read books about this topic.

Emily: Could share her concern with other single moms to see how they have handled similar situations; she could have a mediator work with her ex-husband; she could seek counseling to help her deal with her anger.

Geraldo: Could honestly share his concern with a trusted female relative or friend and ask her to provide some feminine touches to family life; he could seek family counseling to help him deal with his loss and heal.

Jessica: Could ask her pastor or other church staff to recommend another mother or friend to help her with parenting; she could get into a support group for mothers of chronically ill children; she could check into state and local services for single parents.

Point out that it is important for everyone to develop support systems within the extended family and church, as well as in the community. Use the following material with questions to give a short review of the functions of the family.

Do you remember from one of our previous sessions what is the first function of the family? (Love and Nurture.)

We cannot meet all the needs of our family. We can attempt to provide a good place where family members learn about relationships that span generations.

Think for a moment of your own contact as a child with a favorite grandparent, aunt or uncle. What contributions were made to your life through that relationship?

Allow a few moments for responses from the group, noting their points on the chalkboard or newsprint.

Discuss reasons why it is sometimes difficult for families to have contact with grandparents, aunts, uncles, and other relatives.

Suggest the idea of adopted grandparents—older church members become adopted grandparents to children in the church whose grandparents live far away. This idea could also include adopted aunts and uncles, Christian big sisters or brothers, etc.

To put an adopted grandparent (or other) program into

The church as the local expression of the family of God can provide a family experience to its members—young and old.

action, ask a volunteer (or two) in the group to speak to the director of Christian education, Christian education committee, Sunday school superintendent, club coordinator, or other person responsible for programming.

"**Cross-generational interaction is extremely important and will add to the family's nurture base, various role models, and teaching in a variety of skills (shop, house, yard) and commonsense wisdom such as child rearing, marital adjustment, and just plain getting on in the world. Older family members lend experience to all of life's developmental issues. The extended family may also provide physical support and assistance at points of stress. For the single parent the need for these gifts is certainly intensified**" (Brandt and Jackson, 51).

We need to remember that the church as the local expression of the family of God can provide a family experience to its members—young and old.

What is the second family function? (Order and Organization.)

Another way of saying this is that it is the socialization of the family. This is where family members learn their family's life-style and value system. Each family has its own order and organization.

When the isolated nuclear family attempts this on its own, and the world's culture doesn't fit the family's values and patterns, children become confused.

The family must have support of an extended family—preferably the biological and church family. Then, children don't view their "oddball" parent against the whole world, but see two alternative societies. Having Christian values reinforced by other families helps children see the validity of these values. It also helps the single parent feel less alone. The Christian parent doesn't merely make claims of how much better it is to follow the Lord. Instead, there are a variety of examples of how the Christian way is viable, leads to peace, provides love, and is desirable.

Having Christian values reinforced by other families helps children see the validity of these values.

❸ The Treasure of The Church

Objective:
To help single parents explore the potential of the church for being an extended family (10-15 minutes).

How can the church be an extended family? How can it provide the two functions of love and nurture, and order and organization?

Have the participants turn to I John 4:11-13 and ask one person to read the passage aloud. Point out that we know God abides in us when we as a local church provide an extended family environment for the members. It is this love and nurture that provides a basis for making disciples. Sometimes our needs are not met because we do not make them known. Other times people may truly care and recognize a specific need, but are hesitant to reach out because they are not sure what our response will be.

Many parents may have experienced hurt and rejection. They need help to heal. Much of this help should come from the church functioning as family. Pass out copies of "Heavenly Help" (RS-13B). Have a volunteers each read one of the verses aloud and restate God's promise or principle in their own words.

Psalm 27:14—(God will reveal His goodness while I am still living.)
Psalm 55:22—(God will always support me.)
Psalm 71:20—(My problems will not go on forever.)
Psalm 146:9—(God will meet the needs of single families.)
Jeremiah 29:11—(God has good plans for me.)
Nahum 1:7—(God is good and cares for those who trust Him.)
Matthew 11:28—(God will give me rest when I come to Him.)
II Corinthians 1:5—(Christ will comfort me in my sadness.)
II Corinthians 4:16, 17—(God can give inward renewal despite our troubles.)

Point out that God uses other Christians to meet our needs. As someone once said, "The church is God with skin on." God's plan is to meet our needs through the love and nurture we provide for each other in the church.

Hand out copies of "Family Unity" (RS-13C), and have the group find Ephesians 4:25-32 in their Bibles. Ask group members to note the points of order and organization that are mentioned in these verses and to fill in the tasks that God has given Christians and members of His family.

God uses other Christians to meet our needs. As someone once said, "The church is God with skin on."

Verse 25—Speak (truthfully).
Verse 26—In our (anger), do not (sin). Do not (stay angry).
Verse 28—Do not (steal). Work in order to (share).
Verse 29—Avoid (unwholesome) talk. Say what is (helpful).
Verse 31—Get rid of (bitterness).
Verse 32—Be (kind) and (compassionate) to one another.

These verses demonstrate some of the ways that the church provides order and organization—the second function of the church that is similar to an extended family.

❹ Give and Take in God's Family

Objective:
To help parents identify specific ways they could meet each other's needs within the group and throughout the church family (15 minutes).

Hand out copies of "Helping Hands Exchange" (RS-13D). Next to each category shown on the wheel, ask parents to list ways in which he or she needs help.

Give each parent a 3" x 5" index card. Suggest that they select one of the needs they have identified on their sheet of paper and write a "Helping Hands Exchange" ad for it on the card. (Make up an enlarged sample card ahead of time on newsprint and display it.) Provide extra cards for those who would like to make more than one. The task or need should be specific and the exchange offered specific as well.

After you have allowed about five minutes for the creation of cards, have as many participants as possible read their cards to the group. When a person reads a card, they should tack it to the bulletin board, or tape it to the poster board or wall. Later, "takers" can retrieve the cards and make arrangements for the exchange.

Of course, exchanges can be renegotiated from what appears on the cards. Maybe the person willing to fix the screen doors doesn't care much for cherry pies, but could really benefit from having some mending done. So much the better!

Make arrangements ahead of time to put any cards that are not taken on a church bulletin board designated for that purpose or in a special section of the church newsletter so that other church members can be encouraged to respond. Find out how to make this an ongoing practice in your church.

Conclude the course with a time of refreshments and socializing.

As the parents leave, you may wish to give them a duplicated copy of the Bibliography, which has books and publica-

You will forget the shame of your youth and remember no more the reproach of your widowhood."

tions they might want to read for additional help, inspiration, and encouragement. If your church library has any of the books on the list, have them on display and available to check out.

Close with a sentence prayer of thanks for each person in your group.

If parents are interested in further study on parenting, consider the following titles from David C. Cook Publishing Company.

Other Family Growth Electives:
Building Healthy Families by Judson Swihart, Gary Klozenbucher, and Suzan Hawks
Discipline Them, Love Them by Betty N. Chase

LifeTopics Series:
One of a Kind by LaVonne Neff and Anna Trimeiw
The Strong Family by Charles Swindoll and David Sunde
Home Remedies by John Trent, Gary Smalley, and Sue Vanderhook
Keeping Your Teen in Touch with God by Robert Laurent and Dave Jackson

Notes:

1. Yvonne Baker, *Successfully Single* (Denver: Accent Books, 1985), 15.

Bibliography

Aldrich, Sandra P. *From One Single Mother to Another*. Ventura, Calif.: Regal Books, 1992.

Baker, Yvonne G. *Successfully Single*. Denver, Colo.: Accent Books, 1985.

Barnes, Jr., Robert G. *Single Parenting*. Wheaton, Ill.: Tyndale House—Living Books edition, 1992.

Christian Parenting Today Magazine. Sisters, Ore.: Good Family Magazines.

Dobson, Dr. James and Gary L. Bauer, *Children at Risk*. Dallas, Tex.: Word Publishing, 1990.

Falwell, Jerry, *The American Family*. Dallas, Tex: Word Publishing, 1992.

Hansel, Tim, *Through the Wilderness of Loneliness*. Elgin, Ill.: David C. Cook Publishing Co., 1991.

Kesler, Jay, Ron Beers, and LaVonne Neff, editors, *Parents and Children*. Wheaton, Ill.: Victor Books, 1987.

Miller, David R., *Single Moms, Single Dads*. Denver, Colo.: Accent Books, 1990.

Mumford, Amy Ross, *By Death or Divorce . . . It Hurts to Lose*. David C. Cook Publishing Co., 1981.

Murdock, Carol Vejvoda, *Single Parents Are People, Too*. New York: Butterick Publishing, 1980.

Wangerin, Jr., Walter, *Mourning into Dancing*. Grand Rapids, Mich.: Zondervan Publishing House, 1992.

Yancey, Philip, *Disappointment with God*. Grand Rapids, Mich.: Zondervan Publishing House, 1988.

————, *Where Is God When It Hurts?* Grand Rapids, Mich.: Zondervan Publishing House, 1977.

Course Overview

Dates

Single Stories

Story 1:

Arthur is a single father who was not only raised in a Christian home, but whose father was a pastor.

He says, "I was programmed for twenty-fifth and fiftieth wedding anniversaries. I could have handled those nicely. But having to say that I am an 'ex-husband' or a 'divorced man' held a lot of stigma for me."

For him the toughest label is the simple fact that he is "divorced."

Even though the divorce was against his wishes and heartfelt convictions, it happened.

"I didn't have a script for divorce."

Story 2:

Angela, a single mother of three, says that "failure" was the label that hung over her most heavily. A well-meaning friend actually asked her, "Who was wrong? Who sinned in your marriage?"

She was so shocked that she nearly fell out of her chair, but after she recovered, she could only say that she didn't know. For a long time afterward the question echoed in her mind, and she lived with the sense of failure.

Story 3:

Beth Ann, a young widow, said that even though there was no fault attached to her situation, she still had to deal with negative labels. She found that she had to be careful when she was with couples. Because she wasn't part of a couple anymore, she had to be careful that the wrong connotation was not put on her if she joked or was naturally friendly with men. She feared being labeled a "fast woman."

Sticky Situation Studies

Read the following case studies. Identify the negative labels (wrong thinking) the person either has about himself or herself or feels others have about him or her. Locate and read each of the Scriptures to find positive labels (right thinking) the single parents can apply.

Study 1:
Pablo's preteen daughter needs clothing from the inside out (meaning: including lingerie). Pablo hates to shop, knows that both he and his daughter would be embarrassed in the lingerie department, and has no female relatives nearby that he feels comfortable enough to ask for help. (Mom walked out on the family three years ago and is not living in the area.)
    1. How does Pablo feel about himself?
    2. What might the Scriptures below help him to do?

Study 2:
Jasmine received a Thanksgiving food basket from the church this year. She hadn't asked for it; it was just delivered to her home. While money is not plentiful, Jasmine has been able to pay bills and buy food. The gift of food was not a necessity; but it did give the family a few extra dollars that week. When the children saw the food, they asked her if they were on welfare.
    1. How does Jasmine feel about herself?
    2. What might the Scriptures below help her to do?

| Galatians 6:2 | Psalm 68:19 | James 1:17 |
| Ephesians 6:9, 10 | James 1:9 | Ephesians 4:2 |

Your Sticky Situation:

1. How does it make you feel about yourself?

2. What might the Scriptures above help you to do?

Self-Portrait

Part I

Sources of Labels: Parents, Family, Teachers, Peers, Media, Other

- Cut Here - ✀

Part II: A MEMO TO ME

Think about Psalm 139:1-6, 13-16, 23, 24 and respond to the following questions:

1. In a word or two describe what God knows about you.

2. How are you fearfully and wonderfully made? What are your wonderful works (your skills, interests, characteristics, labels, and roles)?

3. Where do you think God is leading you in the next year?

   . . . in the next five years?

4. In what ways might your identity labels be contributing to or hindering what God desires for you?

5. Are you allowing the Identity-Building Cycle to flow and grow? At what steps are you most likely to get stuck? When was the last time you experienced forgiveness?

6. Which parts of your identity enhance you? Which drain your energy and self-esteem? Upon which do you focus most?

The Identity-Building Cycle

1. The identity-building process begins with SELF-KNOWLEDGE. We gather information from many sources—as we've seen in " Self-Portrait" (RS-2A Part I).
    Name one of your labels.

2. Knowing something about ourselves and suspecting a corresponding label usually pushes us to reveal or test this information with someone else. Psychologists call this testing process SELF-DISCLOSURE. We share a part of who we are in a wholesome manner when the sharing takes place within a caring relationship.
    Give an example of when this has happened.

3. The FEEDBACK we receive in the self-disclosure step causes us to affirm, modify, or discard the label we were considering.
    Give an example of when you have affirmed, modified, or discarded a label.

4. If the feedback confirmed a positive label or denied a negative label, we breathe a sigh of relief. But SELF-ACCEPTANCE can also come through confession and receiving God's forgiveness for our sins and failures.
    Give an example of a self-acceptance time.

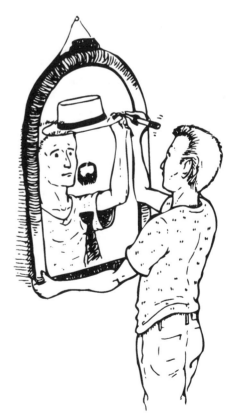

5. Self-acceptance yields GROWTH ENERGY. Of course, the more positive the feedback, the more vigorous the growth energy.
    Give an example of when this has happened to you.

6. GROWTH and CHANGE result as we step out with a new response to life situations.
    Give an example of growth and change in your life.

Me and My Self-Esteem

RS-2C

Part I: KEYS TO CHANGE

1 We need to recognize that esteem building is a lifelong process which happens best with a knowledge of God's love and forgiveness to us. On this foundation the process grows through a series of small steps—most forward, a few backwards. But they always contribute toward expanding our life experience.

2 We must risk new experiences. Lives open to exploration and adventure allow God to shape them.

3 We must be willing to share ourselves, our feelings, our victories, and our defeats with at least one other person in a warm and affirming relationship of mutual support.

Part II: EVALUATION

1. Exploring New Experiences

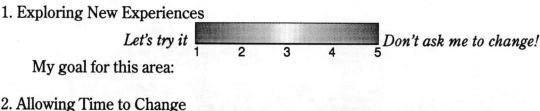

Let's try it 1 2 3 4 5 *Don't ask me to change!*

My goal for this area:

2. Allowing Time to Change

It takes time 1 2 3 4 5 *I expect instant change!*

My goal for this area:

3. Plan in Small Steps

One step at a time 1 2 3 4 5 *All or nothing!*

My goal for this area:

4. Building Warm, Affirming Friendships

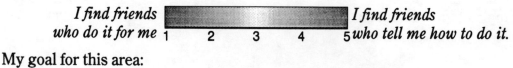

I find friends who do it for me 1 2 3 4 5 *I find friends who tell me how to do it.*

My goal for this area:

What Happened?

Ask two volunteers to read these experiences while others jot down the feelings of the people involved.

I. One single father described his feelings at hearing his wife tell him that she didn't want him to come home anymore as numbness. "This can't happen to me," he recalls. "But then there were the feelings of being rejected as I went through the ugly court battles to try to gain custody of the children.

"I never got to sit down and ask her why, so I never got out from under the feelings of guilt. I always wondered and wondered why? But I'll never know, I guess.

"After that came the anger. Sometimes I would just sit in my office for hours without accomplishing anything productive. It was so hard to admit that I was angry until I was able to accept that it was okay to be angry.

"It was years before I reached the forgiveness and renewal stages.

"I remember one day watching a young couple walking arm and arm and thinking that would never be my experience again. But a few months later I began developing some friend-ships with people who could listen to me, and I could listen to their problems. I suppose it was finding those new relationships and the therapy of talking it out with other people that brought me out of depression."

II. Another single parent described her experience this way:

"My husband had always wanted a son. After having two beautiful baby girls, I found out that he was cheating on me. It was for a short time, and he asked my forgiveness. I loved him—so I took him back.

"I thought that if we had a son, my husband would be happy. Almost immediately, I be-came pregnant. To my delight, the Lord blessed us with a boy. But that was not enough for Joey. Within four months the phone calls started again—if Joey answered, there was someone on the line. If I answered, there was a click and the phone would be dead.

"It didn't take me long to figure out what was happening. After I confronted him, Joey admitted he was seeing someone else. I knew it was true, but could hardly believe it. I was furious. How could he do this to me? To our kids? I was hurt. What was wrong with me? Why did he need another woman? I would have forgiven him again if he had turned around. But no, he filed for divorce and moved in with the other woman. My willingness to forgive turned to hate. I wanted something terrible to happen to that woman.

"I was so scared. How could I raise three children alone? What were the kids supposed to do without a father in the house?

"If it weren't for my closest friend, Janice, I don't know what I would have done. She went to court with me. She cried with me. She brought me to her small group at her church. The women there let me tell my story. They listened and didn't judge me. It helped me know that God still loved me even if my husband didn't."

Beth's Story

Read your assigned part of Beth's story, and decide whether she is in the Denial, Anger/ Bargaining, Depression, or Acceptance stage. Then read the Scripture passage and find parallels between the Bible character's responses and Beth's.

Part I

Beth and Curtis had been married for twenty years and had two children—a preteen and a young elementary daughter. Beth did not want the divorce. On the steps of the court house before the divorce was final, she asked Curtis to reconsider and go with her to counseling. He refused. After the divorce, Curtis continued to visit Beth and the children frequently, often staying for dinner or inviting Beth along when he took the children out. He continued to do small chores and fix-it jobs for Beth. Beth found it was easy to call him to talk about the children and things she needed done such as car maintenance. Even when she knew for sure he was dating her best friend, she and the children made references to Dad coming home.

Scripture: II Samuel 18:19-33. What parallels are evident?

Part II

After several months, Curtis came by less and less and Beth had little reason to call him. She was glad because she didn't want to talk with him while he was dating her best friend steadily and it was rumored that he was going to move in with her. Beth found herself getting into arguments with everyone—the children, her friends, mother, and sister—especially Curtis. She didn't like herself much either and kept asking God, "Why did You let this happen to me?" She was glad Curtis was out of her life and couldn't imagine what she ever saw in him in the first place. She went to the gym to work out three times a week and began dating men at church and in her office, managing to go places where she knew Curtis would see her.

Scripture: John 11:17-32. What parallels are evident?

Part III

A little over a year following the divorce, Curtis married Beth's best friend. Beth went to work, came home, fixed dinner, and went to bed as if on automatic pilot. She talked to the children only when necessary and buried herself in reading and sleeping, ignoring her former interests and hobbies. After several pleas and the urgings of her mother, she went for counseling.

Scripture: I Samuel 1:1-8. What parallels are evident?

Part IV

After two years, Beth began to take a new look at her life. She hardly ever saw Curtis and spoke to him only concerning the children. She applied for a new position in the firm where she worked and started dating one of the men at church regularly. She and the children went on a family vacation and had a wonderful time. When she thinks about the past two years, she feels sad but does not go over every detail of right and wrong as she once did. She feels she's come out on the other side of a shattering experience and is stronger than ever.

Scripture: Job 42:10-17. What parallels are evident?

Here I Am, Lord

Stage	My Typical Behavior	Healing Helps	My Prayer
Denial		Patient listening Frequent reviewing of events of loss Understanding and empathy Little pressure to "face reality"	Psalm 16:1, 11
Anger/Bargaining		Appropriate physical release for anger A "sounding board" to listen Little pressure to calm down	Psalm 94
Depression		Maintain regular routines and exercise Free expression of grief and mourning Emotional release Counseling	Psalm 30
Acceptance		New goals and outlets Assistance with refocusing plans Physical and emotional outlets	Psalm 118

This Is Reality

Part I

All of us from the time we were little children have been socialized to think of life—particularly _____ _____—as something to be done in _____. Thus, we feel a mixture of _____ when faced with prospect of being a single parent/head of household.

Our feelings range from _____ and_____ to _____and _____. For women especially, there is often a fear of _____ and _____. After all, isn't it risky to become too able to care for oneself? To be _____ is often thought of as needing to be _____ and _____. If these dependencies are gone, then what of the _____? If one does not _____ someone else, then maybe there _____ anyone else!

Much the same is true for many men. The thought of making it alone is not_____, not _____, not_____. And this is understandable. God did not intend_____ _____ to be handled by one parent alone. God said, "It is not good for man to be _____. I will make a _____ suitable for him." And certainly the same is true for women, especially when their task is _____.

For those who have been married, the _____ of husband or wife is not merely the loss of the _____ and _____ of a mate. It is a loss of a _____—the _____ of wife or husband. As such, it is the loss of a major part of one's_____ and often a source of one's _____. Thus, the prospect of _____ a life alone and a family life as a single adult brings out all sorts of feelings.

However, even though single parenthood is not the _____, it is the _____for those of us in this group. And it is important to _____ it.

Part II

"O Lord, our God, we confess that often we do not like the bodies we have. Sometimes we have longed for jobs of others. We would like to do away with parts of our history. We are afraid of our moods and feelings. We wish we had more time. We would like to start over again. We lust after the prestige of others. We think more money will solve our problems. We resent the injustices we have suffered and cherish our sorrows. We want to be appreciated for our small graces. We are enchanted by the past and enticed by the future. We have never really been understood. In short, we have refused to live because we have held out for better terms. Heal us, O God, from the distance we have tried to put between ourselves and life. Restore to us the love of thee and all creation. Enable us by thy power to be renewed in our whole lives, through Jesus Christ our Lord, Amen."

—*Helmut Thielicke*

First Steps Contract

List your three top priorities in terms of your family.

1.

2.

3.

Consider each of the areas of your life that are listed below. In the first column place a check if you've seen progress in the past six months. Choose three areas where you would like to see progress in the next six months. In the middle column, list one goal for each of these areas. In the far right-hand column identify any obstacles and potential solutions related to each goal.

	Areas Where I've Seen Growth	Areas Needing Progress/Goals	Obstacles/ Solutions
Spiritual			
Job/Career			
Physical			
Social			
Management			
Income			
Homemaking			
Maintenance			
Other			

Select ONE of the areas mentioned above, the one you think is most IMMEDIATELY attainable. Fill in the following contract in terms of that goal.

I, _____, have decided to increase my competence in_____, by working toward the specific goal of being able to_____. The first step I must take to accomplish this is to identify my present way of functioning in this area. It could be described as _____.

In a similar situation I hope to be able to _____.

I will begin to develop this new competence by _____

I will know some progress has been made when I observe that _____ and I will report that progress to my partner _____.

Signed, _____ date _____

Signed, _____ date _____

Ways Kids Cope

Read the following case studies and identify which phase(s) of loss—protest, anger, or hope—each child is demonstrating.

Case Study A: Michael is fifteen months old. His mother and father are recently divorced, and his mother is in the hospital. His father works two jobs and has little time for the toddler. The baby-sitter is loving but Michael seems withdrawn. He sits with a sad expression and is difficult to draw into play. He is not interested in eating but is passive in his resistance to mealtimes. He is not passive at bedtimes, though. He resists vigorously—screaming and crying. This seems to be the only time of day that he has any energy.

Case Study B: Jeff is twelve years old and resistant to any suggestions. He often clearly does the opposite of what he is asked, both at home and at school. Several of his possessions are broken and he seems to have lots of minor "accidents." He has gotten into a number of arguments and fights with friends and siblings.

Case Study C: Tanya is age six. She recently asked her mother to take her past the house where they used to live before the divorce. After they returned home, she told her mother she was going to choose some clothes and toys that she could leave in her daddy's apartment for when she spent weekends with him.

Case Study D: Mario, age eight, covered his ears when his mother and father told him of their plans to get a divorce. Later in the week he came home from play and called out, "Dad, Dad, are you home? Can we play ball?" Even though he knows his dad has moved out, he keeps his ball, mitt, and bat beside the back door ready for Dad to come home.

Case Study E: Samantha has just turned thirteen. She is happy that her mother left the family. "Now all that nagging and yelling is gone too," she reminds anyone who will listen. On the afternoon of her birthday Samantha was home alone and she threw out all of her mother's things. When the rest of the family returned home, she had prepared supper and a cake.

Three Phases of Loss for Children

RS-5B

1. Protest—In this phase the child is dealing with the shock of the loss. Just as in the adult loss cycle, when the first reaction is to shut down emotionally and sometimes physically, children may do the same. They may become passive, cuddle with cherished blankets or stuffed animals, want to be held, or refuse to eat. All of this may alternate with a panic reaction. Loss heightens the child's sense of vulnerability.

As the child sees it, his or her very safety and well-being is at stake. Panic reactions include protests at being put to bed and difficulty in going to sleep, separation anxiety, reluctance in going to school or going to play with a friend. Physical problems such as rashes, allergies, and bronchial infections are common.

Later in the protest phase the child may deny the loss, respond with hyperactivity, reject the very one who has been lost, search for the lost ones, become excessively disorganized, or cling to a dream of a fairy-tale reunion.

2. Anger—In the anger phase, the child is facing and working through the deep hurt of the loss which has impacted his or her life. Again, the child will tend to do grief work through his or her behavior rather than through words. Anger is particularly difficult for children to express openly because it often leads to further trouble. Sometimes they are afraid of anger because of its intense power and potential destructiveness. The child imagines that his or her own fury may cause more loss, punishment, revenge, abandonment, or even death. Finally, a child may get the message—intended or otherwise—that anger and sadness are not permitted in the family.

Behaviorally, children's anger may result in an increased number of "accidents" to themselves, their toys, and those around them. They may bully and fight; they may resist; they may passively resist; they may argue and complain; they may continue to display hyperactive and disorganized behavior. They may also develop further physical symptoms such as vomiting, asthma, or severe headaches.

In contrast to these behaviors the child could also become the "perfect" child—compulsively adhering to all rules.

Of course, none of these symptoms alone is an indicator of how the child is doing. Most children resist, argue, and complain sometimes and, hopefully, obey most of the time. But what is significant to the processing of loss is a marked change in the child's behavior or the child's functioning at one or the other ends of the behavior spectrum.

3. Hope—After anger, the child moves on to the good-bye process. In cases of gradual loss there is time to actually say good-bye. In cases of sudden or unresolved loss (death, abandonment, or difficult custody battles) the child must symbolically say good-bye.

This letting-go process may be in the form of a visit to old places; it may be a letter, tape, or drawing. It could be a photo album or even a drama replayed with dolls and toys. The saying good-bye step is essential to the loss cycle. Without it the child will not be free to say hello to new situations and relationships. This is the key to an attitude of hope.

Lost and Found

Below are listed some of the common symptoms for the three stages of children's response to loss.

PLEASE NOTE: Remember that most kids exhibit some of these things. What you need to look for in your child is patterns, extremes, or sudden changes in behavior.

PROTEST	**ANGER**	**HOPE**
Passive responses	Resistance	Good-byes
Difficult bedtimes	Fighting	Hellos
Denial	Mourning	Plans for the future
Yearning/searching	Perfect behavior	(holidays, vaca-
Rejecting	Accidents	tions, school, etc.)
Hyperactivity	Physical symptoms	
Disorganization	Self-abuse	

On the left, list your child's name (duplicate the chart on the back of this sheet or on additional paper for each child). Under each of the three headings identify the behaviors you currently observe. Finally, fill in plans for helping each child in his or her journey to hope.

	Protest	**Anger**	**Hope**
Name: _____ Plans for help:			

WHEN TO SEEK PROFESSIONAL HELP

- When troubled behavior persists longer than a month or two.
- When behavior is consistently below age appropriateness.
- When low self-esteem is reflected in self-depreciation and/or self-injury.
- When a physical motion or pattern is repeated compulsively.
- When play is always or never alone.
- When a behavioral change is sudden and interferes with day-to-day living.
- When the child complains of ongoing pain with no obvious physical origin.
- When there is consistent aggressive behavior.
- When a child falls apart every time he or she makes a mistake.
- When a child is always good.

God's Promises for My Family

RS-5D

Share one verse each week or two with your family. You might discuss what the verse means and write a prayer for your family in the space provided.

Psalm 9:9, 10

Psalm 27:1

Psalm 34:4

Psalm 46:1

Psalm 50:14, 15

Psalm 56:3, 4

Psalm 147:3

Matthew 5:4

Matthew 11:28

John 14:27

Romans 8:28

I Peter 5:7

A Slogan That Fits Me

1. You've Come a Long Way, Baby!

2. M'M! M'M! Good!

3. You're Looking Smarter Than Ever!

4. Powerful Good!

5. Performance Counts!

6. I'm Worth It!

7. Every Day Should Feel This Good!

8. Be All You Can Be

9. I'm Tickled Pink!

10. Always a Step Ahead!

11. Just Do It!

12. Oh! What a Feeling!

13. You're in Good Hands

14. The Power to Be Your Best

15. It's More Than Tough.
    It's Unbeatable!

It's All in How You Say It!

Ask questions that expand, not constrict.

"Tell me more about that."
"What did you feel then?"
"Would you like to tell me about it?"
"I'm wondering if . . . ?"

Restate feelings and issues.

"I hear you saying . . ."
"Are you feeling . . . ?"
"You want me to . . ."

Affirm both being and doing.

"I'm glad you are here."
"That must have been hard."
"I enjoy being with you."
"You're good at that."
"You are important to me."
"Thank you for doing . . ."

Family Portrait

Love and Nurture:

Order and Organization:

Vision for Family:

What Is the Function?

Look up the Scriptures assigned to you and write down a key word or summary word of the family function that is mentioned. Then check off whether it is a love-and-nurture, an order-and-organization, or a vision-for-family function.

	Key/Summary Word	Love and Nurture	Order and Organization	Vision for Family
Genesis 2:24				
Exodus 20:12				
Deuteronomy 6:1-7				
Deuteronomy 24:5				
Psalm 68:3-6				
Psalm 103:13				
Proverbs 1:8, 9				
Proverbs 4:1-4				
Matthew 19:4-9				
Colossians 3:18-21				
Ephesians 6:1-4				
I Peter 3:1-8				
I John 4:11, 12				

Building Blocks

LOVE AND NURTURE

1 **Giving and Receiving Love**
How do you tell family members they are loved?
How do you encourage family members to show love to one another?

2 **Developing Communication Skills**
What do you do to encourage family members to talk to one another?
How do you train family members to discuss their needs?

3 **Growing Emotionally**
How are feelings handled in your family?
What do you do to encourage the expression and healthy control of feelings?
How do you celebrate happy events and remember sad ones?

4 **Handling Power**
How do you train family members for independence and responsibility?
How are decisions made in the family?

ORDER AND ORGANIZATION

1 **Socialization and Discipline**
How do you train family members in the roles of life, such as student,
    employee, parent, child, male, female?
What special traditions do you use to help family members feel they belong?

2 **Christian Values-Building**
What values are important in the family?
How can these be built into the lives of family members?

VISION FOR FAMILY

1 **"We're Okay, but Not Ideal"**
How do you affirm that your family is "okay"—with God's help—without
    suggesting that the single parent model is an option your kids can select?
What do you do to deliberately teach the biblical ideal of two parents?

2 **Drawing on Other Families**
Name some two-parent families you could expose your children to.
Which two-parent families in your family tree could you tell your children about?

Your Energy Bank

RS-8A

Read through the list; then go back to rate each item. Record the impact each activity has on your energy level. Place a number under both columns—Debit and Credit—to indicate what it takes out of you and what it gives back to you. The scale for Debits is 0 to -3 and for Credits is 0 to +3. Record all your scores before calculating the Net Result. Determine the Net Result for each activity by adding the scores in the two columns.

	How much it takes out of me Debit (-) -3 -2 -1 0	How much I get out of doing it Credit (+) 0 +1 +2 +3	Debits +Credits = Net Result
Earning a living			
Spending time with the children			
Helping with homework			
Having daily prayer/devotions			
Maintaining the car			
Doing the shopping			
Going to church			
Planning meals			
Preparing			
Setting limits			
Enforcing rules			
Leading family devotions			
Taking a night out with friends			
Reading for recreation			
Doing home maintenance			
Transporting the children to activities			
Participating in a sport or hobby			
Keeping an even temper			
Scheduling time for things you enjoy			
Being strong and stable for the kids			
Settling arguments			
Reading to the children			
Hugging and cuddling the children			
Managing the budget			
Exercising regularly			
Feeling guilty about unmet expectations			
Making major purchases			
Planning vacations			
Celebrating holidays			
Relating to ex-spouse			
Serving in ministry to others			
Having company			

Add the Net Result column to determine your ENERGY BALANCE .... _____

Don't let your score surprise or alarm you. This is not a precise tool. It can give you an idea of your energy reserves and whether or not you are trying to be a superparent.

Tough or Tender

"Be humble and gentle. Be patient with each other, making allowance for each other's faults because of your love" (Ephesians 4:2, The Living Bible).

	Too Tough	Too Tender
Child's name		
Child's name		
Child's name		
Child's name		

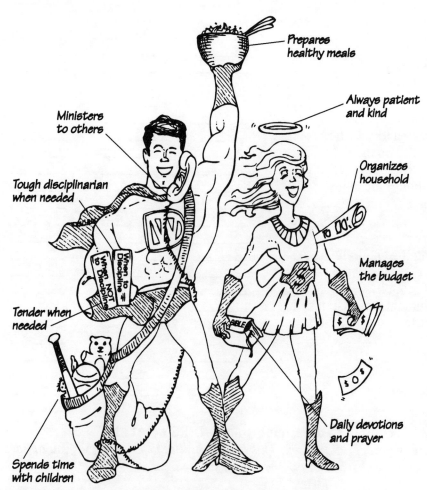

Letting Trust Grow

Roleplay #1:

Sally is a single mom with custody of her two boys. Her ex-husband is dating a woman and often has her spend the night, even when the boys are visiting. Sally is fearful that the boys' moral training is being undermined by their father's example in this area and others.

Roleplay #2:

Claudia has custody of her seven-year-old daughter, Summer. Summer's dad Jose deserted the family when she was only six months old. Providing for Summer has been a constant challenge for Claudia. Jose had no contact with Claudia or Summer until about a year ago. At that time, he called and asked if he could see Summer. Since then he has been giving her expensive gifts and taking her to local amusement parks, etc. Claudia is fearful that Summer views Jose as fun, while she sees Claudia as dull. It almost feels as if some kind of contest is going on about who's the best parent.

Roleplay #3:

Jack has been a single dad for eight years—ever since Sylvia left him with their three young children. Jack has custody of the kids, who are now thirteen, eleven, and nine. To keep the household running smoothly, he has had to establish and enforce high standards and a spirit of teamwork. The children all have age-appropriate chores and are expected to follow the household rules. When they visit their mother every other weekend they do not have to help out at all. The kids report that Mom tells them that their dad is too strict and even abusive. Jack fears that the children will want to live with their mom.

Roleplay #4:

Jeremy and his ex-wife, Izzie, have been divorced for only six months and have joint custody of their fourteen-year-old son, Arthur. Izzie has already remarried, and Jeremy is quickly getting tired of hearing Arthur's admiration of his new stepdad, Marcus. When Arthur referred to Marcus as dad, Jeremy felt like he had been punched. From the reports that Jeremy is getting, he is wondering if Arthur's loyalties are changing. This coming weekend Arthur and his stepdad are going camping together, which is something Arthur had been requesting for a long time. Somehow Jeremy never quite found the time to plan such a trip. Now he is wondering if he has made a big mistake.

Trust or Consequences

Select one or more responses which you feel will strengthen the trust bond between parent and child or share one you feel will work better—perhaps from your own experience!

1. Miguel, age ten, is a strong defender of his father, even though his dad appears late or not at all for visitation times. Miguel's frustrated mother should . . .
   a. Tell Miguel she doesn't want to hear anymore about his father.
   b. Try to make Miguel's father understand how disappointing his inconsistency is to Miguel.
   c. Allow Miguel to work out his own relationship with his dad.
   d. Your suggestion:

2. Joanie leaves her bike unlocked on the front porch although she has been warned not to do so. The day before the bike hike with the junior high youth group, the bike is stolen. Joanie's father should . . .
   a. Give Joanie a loan to buy a new bike.
   b. Sympathize with Joanie concerning her loss.
   c. Suggest that Joanie rent or borrow a bike for the trip.
   d. Tell Joanie it is her fault, and she'll have to save to get a bike for herself.
   e. Your suggestion:

3. Three-year-old Angela is afraid of the dark. She often refuses to go to bed. Her father is having a difficult time coping with this new fear. She was such a confident child before her mother died. He should . . .
   a. Purchase a night-light and sit quietly on the bed for a few minutes after goodnight prayers.
   b. Take care to establish a consistent bedtime routine.
   c. Encourage Angela to talk about the loss of her mother.
   d. Insist that Angela go to bed and stop making such a fuss.
   e. Your suggestion:

4. Robert's mother would like him to sleep through the night now that he is twenty months old. But he has recently been waking up more often—five or six times a night—demanding to get up and eat and wailing when he can't. His mother should . . .
   a. Get some earplugs, close the doors, and ignore him.
   b. Feed him as he demands, hoping he will grow out of the stage.
   c. Go to him to assure him of her presence, maybe putting him back down and patting his back, but refusing to get him up or feed him.
   d. Call his father and tell him that Robert is entering the terrible twos early and she can't cope.
   e. Your suggestion:

5. Timmy, age six, wants to go to the neighborhood playground by himself. It is only two blocks away and in a safe area. Even so, his mom does not feel Timmy is old enough to play unsupervised. She should . . .
   a. Tell him he can't go unless she goes with him.
   b. Tell Timmy he can go alone when he is older. Then tell him he can go to the play area with an older friend from the neighborhood for a specified amount of time.
   c. Let him go even though she is uneasy about it.
   d. Your suggestion:

Trust—The Bond That Ties

Fill this worksheet out for each of your children. Use the back of this sheet or additional paper as needed.

Child's name/age	Next appropriate area of trust	I find release difficult because . . .	One smaller step I could try is . . .

Just Checking

The goal for adults: intimacy—to develop skills in sharing oneself in deep relationships. To learn to give, care, share, and sacrifice for others.

To achieve this goal, we must take care of ourselves and manage our lives well. Rate yourself in terms of each of the criteria listed below. Remember: We are all still growing. God isn't done with any of us yet! (Aren't you glad?)

4 = Doing great!
3 = Making good progress!
2 = Need some improvement.
1 = Hope no one is peeking!

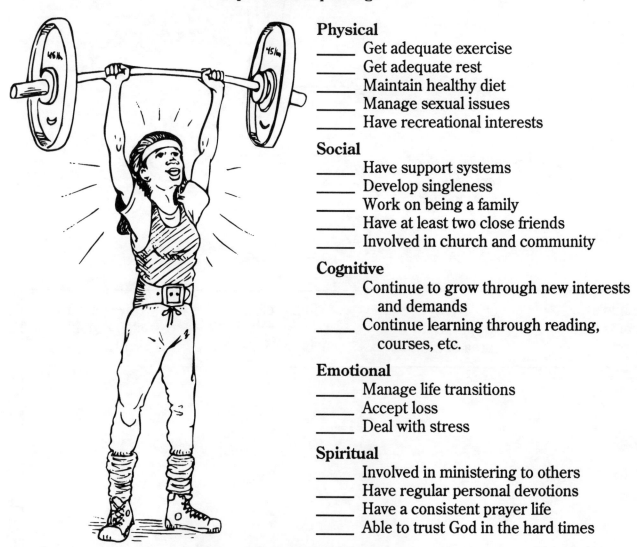

Physical
_____ Get adequate exercise
_____ Get adequate rest
_____ Maintain healthy diet
_____ Manage sexual issues
_____ Have recreational interests

Social
_____ Have support systems
_____ Develop singleness
_____ Work on being a family
_____ Have at least two close friends
_____ Involved in church and community

Cognitive
_____ Continue to grow through new interests
       and demands
_____ Continue learning through reading,
       courses, etc.

Emotional
_____ Manage life transitions
_____ Accept loss
_____ Deal with stress

Spiritual
_____ Involved in ministering to others
_____ Have regular personal devotions
_____ Have a consistent prayer life
_____ Able to trust God in the hard times

Circle the category with the lowest score. What can you realistically do to change this area over the next three to six months?

How Do Your Children Grow?

As a group, read through the developmental tasks appropriate to the stage of your child. Rate each task for your child in the following way:

> **3 = made it**
> **2 = almost there**
> **1 = needs some help**

Infant Goal: Trust   Name of child _____

To develop security through physical comfort as physical needs are met in predictable patterns.

Physical	*Social*	*Cognitive*	*Emotional*
____Cries	____Attaches to family	____Experiments with	____Feels secure when
____Grasps things	members	cause and effect	needs are met
____Reaches for things	____Smiles	____Beginning to master	
____Holds things	____Babbles	physical body	
____Sits up	____Says words		
____Crawls			
____Takes steps			

Toddler Goal: Autonomy   Name of child _____

To develop an I-can-do-it-myself confidence through increased mastery of physical skills.

Physical	*Social*	*Cognitive*	*Emotional*
____Feeds self	____Takes part in	____Beginning to	____Begins to under-
____Can dress and	parallel play	understand	stand free-
undress	(alongside other	language	dom within limits
____Runs	toddlers)	____Can make two-	____Begins to make
____Climbs stairs	____Says, "no"	word sentences	appropriate
____Throws things	____Says, "I can do it"	____Very literal	choices
____Jumps		____Can distinguish	
____Begins toilet		male from female	
training		____Beginning to un-	
		derstand rules	
		____Connects disobedi-	
		ence to negative	
		consequences	

(Continued on next resource sheet)

How Do Your Children Grow? (cont'd.)

Preschool Goal: Initiative   Name of child _____

To develop an increased sense of separateness through making independent choices.

Physical	*Social*	*Cognitive*	*Emotional*
_____Climbs	_____Begins to attach to same sex	_____Talks a lot	_____Understands freedom to initiate when given clear structure
_____Rides tricycle	_____Loves opposite sex parent	_____Can say whole sentences	
_____Hops	_____Egocentric but will play with other children	_____Understands more concepts	
_____Swings		_____Enjoys pretending	
_____Can perform simple chores such as picking up toys or clothes, emptying the trash, etc.		_____Understands rules, rewards and consequences	
		_____Can count	

Elementary Goal: Industry   Name of child _____

To develop the special skills and talents which increase competence at home and away.

Physical	*Social*	*Cognitive*	*Emotional*
_____Skips	_____Plays and shares with others	_____Able to save money for special purpose	_____Beginning to have competence based on accomplishment of skills
_____Jumps rope	_____Attached to same sex role model	_____Academic skills are getting better	
_____Throws	_____Enjoys hobbies and sports	_____Knows and follows rules	
_____Hits a small ball	_____Likes groups and clubs	_____Able to follow instructions	
_____Kicks	_____Has a best friend		
_____Has artistic ability			
_____Can do complex chores such as cooking, laundry, bed-making			

Adolescent Goal: Identity   Name of child _____

To develop an integrated and independent sense of self, separate from family but related to friends.

Physical	*Social*	*Cognitive*	*Emotional*
_____Body is growing rapidly	_____Shares friendships	_____Thinks abstractly/ symbolically	_____Experiments with a variety of roles from a secure base
_____Beginning sexual maturity	_____Interested in opposite sex	_____Learning about roles in life	_____Has frequent emotional turmoil as new things are explored.
_____Has pimples	_____Dates	_____Has the ability to see another's point of view	
_____Can do household chores independently	_____Involved in independent activities	_____Fantasizes about future goals	
	_____Can take leadership	_____Learning to manage money	
	_____Works outside of family		

Next Steps

1. Child's name:

2. Developmental stage:

3. List any tasks the child still needs to master in this stage:

    Put a star by any tasks that your child is ready to attempt.

4. Select one task listed in Step 3 that you would like to help your child work on right away.

5. As a group, brainstorm ways to help your child take the first small step toward the goal in Step 4. Record any ideas you like:

6. What will you need to do this next week to get things started?

Created in His Image

Look up and use the contents of your assigned verses to write an acrostic that highlights some of the similarities and differences between men and women. For each letter listed below, use one verse (or set of two verses) to write a sentence or phrase that describes how men and women are either the same or different. You may use the verses in any order and the bold letters may appear anywhere in your sentence.

Group I: Genesis 2:7, 22; Exodus 35:22; Proverbs 31:29 and Isaiah 32:8; Isaiah 38:19; Luke 8:1-3; Acts 4:32.

Group II: Numbers 18:7; Joshua 1:14; Ezra 10:1; Acts 5:14; I Corinthians 11:11; Ephesians 5:21, 25, 33.

M

E

N

W

O

M

E

N

So What's the Difference?

The last two differences are less pronounced than others. They show up statistically, but any individual may cross over. Obviously, experience, personality, and culture contribute significantly to some differences.

<table>
<tr><td>

Males
Ordained distinct (Gen. 1:27)
Every cell masculine
(XY chromosomes)

</td><td>

Females
Ordained distinct (Gen. 1:27)
Every cell feminine
(XX chromosomes)

</td></tr>
</table>

Males	Females
• Men can be fathers.	• Women can be mothers.
• Because males have larger muscles, slight differences in bone structure, and a better oxygen delivery system, they tend to be stronger, faster, and more agile.	• Women tend to excel in certain endurance tests because they are more flexible. They seem to have more tolerance for pain and develop earlier, both physically and mentally.
• Males are more susceptible to some physical and emotional diseases.	• Women seem to have more problems with depression.
• Fewer males are born, and their life expectancy is shorter.	• More females are born, and they live longer.
• In general, males are more spatially oriented and more aggressive.	• Females are usually more intuitive and more verbal.

Many characteristics
are determined by
family heredity,
experience, personality,
and culture.

Three Components of Self-Esteem

RS-11C

Sense of Worth = *"I am loved." Both parents can provide this.*
Sense of Adequacy = *"I can do it." Same-sex parent contributes most.*
Sense of Identity = *"I belong, and I am unique." Both parents provide assurance of belonging. Both parents can reinforce basic uniqueness. However, part of uniqueness is sexual identity. The same-sex parent provides a model. The opposite-sex parent affirms progress toward that ideal.*

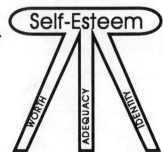

Once a child knows his or her gender, there is the ongoing discovery of what that means. Again there is a role for both fathers and mothers. When a boy is developing an image of what it means to be a man, he will most likely look to his father as a model. Similarly, when a girl is establishing what it means to be a woman, she will look to the example of her mother.

According to marriage and family counselors, sexual identity is most effectively affirmed by the opposite-sex parent.

The same-sex parents provides the model; the opposite-sex parent affirms progress toward that ideal.

There are two additional tasks that a father normally accomplishes in the two-parent family. He helps his son separate from the protective skirts of the mother in a way that encourages his adventuresome manhood. This separation also prepares him to be able to love another woman—his future wife. The task with the daughter is slightly different. The father is the first male she falls in love with. For her, these new and important feelings are the seeds for a fulfilling marriage. A good father both nurtures and then redirects them. Emotionally, he communicates, "It's not me; I belong to your mother. But someday there will be a husband whom you can love and give yourself to fully."

Though this may happen somewhat automatically in most two-parent families, even some two-parent families have difficulty reinforcing the sexual identity of their children if the parents do not understand these functions and work to fulfill them.

The wise single parent can compensate with careful planning. First, we must understand the importance for our children of regular contact with loving and trustworthy adults of both sexes. Second, we must concentrate on the aspects of the developmental process we can do best. Third, we must get help in the tasks we cannot perform.

In these ways we can be competent single parents.

A child's need to have ongoing contact with loving adults of both sexes is sometimes the most important reason to maintain contact with the noncustodial parent, if possible.

Fill in the chart below with the things that mothers and fathers can do to build the sexual identity of their sons and daughters.

WHAT EACH PARENT PROVIDES BEST

	Mother	Father
Sons		
Daughters		

What I Can Do Best

Child's Name	In terms of sexual identity, I can help . . .	A person of the opposite sex is needed to help . . .	Possible candidates

Tips for Getting Help:

1. State reason clearly.
2. Use caution. Follow your instincts.
3. Separate dating relationships and role models.
4. Guard your emotions.

Have You Tried This Adventure?

Check any activities on this list that you would like to try. Write down any new ideas that are mentioned by the group and sound interesting to you.

bowling	visiting museums
tennis	touring and sightseeing
hiking	trying a new art form
water skiing	biking
swimming	swap meets
scuba diving	jogging
racquetball	picnics
table games	ball games
fishing	attending dog shows
camping	attending flower shows
classes	mountain climbing
gardening	day trips
carpentry	photography
horseback riding	sailing
visiting relatives	trips to the library
concerts	plays
garage sales	roller blading

_____ _____

_____ _____

_____ _____

_____ _____

_____ _____

_____ _____

Picking Up Dropped Stitches

Part I—With the Children

SITUATIONS	RISKS	SOLUTIONS
Camping for the first time with your three grade-school-age children.		
Attending your first family reunion without a spouse.		
Your nine-year-old son begs you to take him to a football game. You've never been to one, and you are sure you won't like it.		
Attending church family functions such as picnics, potlucks, family camp, etc. without a spouse.		
Giving a sleep-over birthday party for one of your children.		

Part II—With Other Adults

SITUATIONS	RISKS	SOLUTIONS
You've decided it is time to get involved at church and to meet some new friends. The adult Single Parent's Group has a hayride and cookout planned for two weeks from tomorrow.		
A single man at work is very attractive to you. He invites you to his home for dinner with friends. After the friends leave . . .		
You want to go on the weekend retreat with your small group from church, but everyone else in the group is married. You fear that in many activities and discussions you will feel left out.		
Two single parents have been dating each other for a year. One of them is eager to marry and the other isn't.		

Why Do I Feel This Way?

1. Sexual feelings are normal and a part of being a physical human. They do not stop simply because one has become single.

2. We all have a need to be touched, held, and comforted. These needs for physical intimacy are often intensified in periods of emotional stress, but they can also generate sexual feelings. Try to plan for alternative ways in which these needs can be at least partially met. What are some alternative ways (such as hugging the children more)?
What else?

3. What we see, touch, and hear can arouse sexual feelings. Try to avoid situations that arouse this energy for which there is not adequate outlet at this time. However, don't become too anxious. Exercise, particularly regular fitness activities, also helps.

4. Sexual feelings are partially emotional intimacy. Emotional intimacy is the sharing of an experience of deeply felt empathy and concern. Intimacy is the exchange of love when the needs of the other are as important as your needs. It is friendship at its deepest. Try to cultivate one or two friendships at a deep level of intimacy without any physical involvement. Often these will be with another of the same sex. Enjoy these as one of the benefits of being single.

Write I Corinthians 6:13, 18-20 in your own words.

Read I Corinthians 10:13, 14. Write a contract with God concerning your sexual feelings.

I, _____, hereby agree to

Help! Case Studies

1. Zack is a widower and the sole support of two young children. He has a job that he does not enjoy, but it is the only one for which he has skills. Each month, by the time he pays child care, rent, food, and a few other bills, he is broke.

2. Steven, age seven and the youngest of three children, is very interested in his fourteen-year-old sister's nail polish, hair curlers, and pretty dresses. He also plays with her discarded Barbie dolls. Steven's mother and father are divorced, and Steven has only limited contact with his dad. Steven's older brother Douglas, age sixteen, has a hard time relating positively to Steven.

3. Ryan, age eight, is having difficulty in school. Not only is his behavior inappropriate, but his learning is slow. He has difficulty concentrating and is not interested in learning. His mother Joanne is discouraged and has a lot of trouble helping him at home as the teacher has suggested. She begins okay, but soon loses patience. Yelling, nagging, and lecturing begin. As much as possible, Joanne avoids the teacher. That way she doesn't have to hear about and get discouraged over Ryan.

4. Emily is furious with her ex-husband, Sam. His support payments are always late and insufficient. She is living on less than half their previous income and is having increasing trouble meeting basic expenses. She is making it harder for Sam to see the children because she doesn't think he deserves to see them. In response, he is more reluctant to pay his share of the child support.

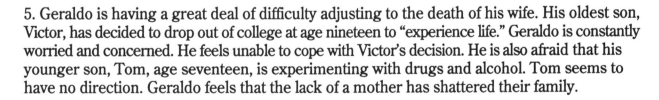

5. Geraldo is having a great deal of difficulty adjusting to the death of his wife. His oldest son, Victor, has decided to drop out of college at age nineteen to "experience life." Geraldo is constantly worried and concerned. He feels unable to cope with Victor's decision. He is also afraid that his younger son, Tom, age seventeen, is experimenting with drugs and alcohol. Tom seems to have no direction. Geraldo feels that the lack of a mother has shattered their family.

6. Jessica is young and unmarried and the mother of a preemie. The infant is now at home but needs constant care and watching. The baby needs to be fed every two hours and should be participating in an infant stimulation program. Jessica is on welfare and has not yet finished high school. She is feeling far from loving toward the infant. Anger, frustration, and isolation are her dominant feelings.

Heavenly Help

Wait for the Lord; be strong and take heart and wait for the Lord.
　　　　—Psalm 27:14

The Lord watches over the alien and sustains the fatherless and the widow, but he frustrates the ways of the wicked.
　　　　—Psalm 146:9

"Come to me, all you who are weary and burdened, and I will give you rest."
　　　　—Matthew 11:28

Cast your cares on the Lord and he will sustain you; he will never let the righteous fall.
　　　　—Psalm 55:22

"For I know the plans I have for you," declares the Lord, "plans to prosper you and not to harm you, plans to give you hope and a future."
　　　　—Jeremiah 29:11

For just as the sufferings of Christ flow over into our lives, so also through Christ our comfort overflows.
　　　　—II Corinthians 1:5

Though you have made me see troubles, many and bitter, you will restore my life again; from the depths of the earth you will again bring me up.
　　　　—Psalm 71:20

The Lord is good, a refuge in times of trouble.
He cares for those who trust in him.
　　　　—Nahum 1:7

Therefore do not lose heart. Though outwardly we are wasting away, yet inwardly we are being renewed day by day.
　　　　—II Corinthians 4:16

Family Unity

In Ephesians, the apostle Paul is affirming the nature of the church. In chapter four, he talks about what it means to be part of the body of Christ—the church. When we are in Christ, we are joined together with other believers in a family relationship.

In Ephesians 4:25-32, note the ways that the church is to fulfill the family function of encouraging order and organization between people in the church.

Verse	Task	Function
25	Speak _____.	Enhances order
26	In our _____, do not _____.	Preserves order
26b	Do not _____ _____.	Restores order
28	Do not _____.	Creates order
28b	Work in order to _____.	Develops caring organization
29	Avoid _____ talk.	Preserves order
29b	Say what is _____.	Enhances organization
31	Get rid of _____.	Protects order
32	Be _____ and _____ to one another.	Such organization extends Christ's love

Helping Hands Exchange

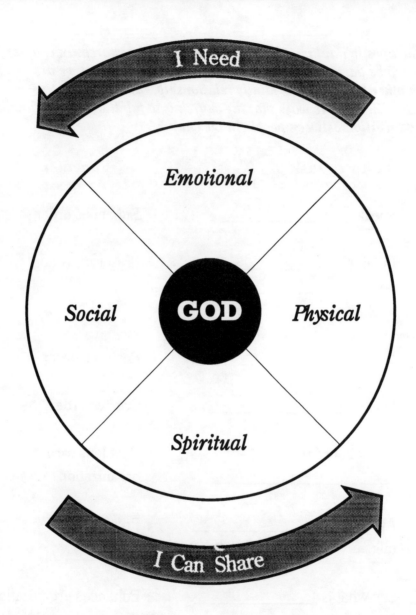

One *HOMEMADE CHERRY PIE* in exchange for repairing my screen door —555-5555, Joanne

LAWN MAINTENANCE in exchange for Saturday morning child care — 555-1111, Doug